AN ORDINARY PERSON

WITH AN

EXTRAORDINARY GOD

Suzanne Ross

An Ordinary Person
with an
Extraordinary God

Suzanne Ross

SHOSHANNAH MINISTRIES

DB

DIADEM BOOKS

An Ordinary Person with an Extraordinary God

Published by Diadem Books
An imprint of Spiderwize

For information, please contact:

Diadem Books
Mews Cottage
The Causeway
KENNOWAY
The Kingdom of Fife
KY8 5JU

www.diadembooks.com

ISBN: 978-1-907294-68-6

Unless otherwise indicated, scriptures are from the NIV (New International Version).

Jesus said in a loud voice: "If anyone is thirsty, let him come to me and drink. Whoever believes in me, as the Scripture has said, streams of living water will flow from within him."

John 7:38

AUTHOR'S NOTE

The cover depicts a drip of water about to break the surface on a beautiful clear blue lake. There are already a few ripples spreading out in ever increasing circles from previous drips.

My book is made up of personal testimonies about the mighty works of God. I pray each story…each chapter…may be like the small drip on a big lake, but the accumulative effect is the spreading of the Good News of the Gospel of Jesus Christ further and further afield.

Many years ago God gave me the words – SHOSHANNAH MINISTRIES. *Shoshannah* is Hebrew for my name Suzanne and means Lily of Testimony. I actually saw it written in the water one day with the drip…but that's another story!

Suzanne Ross

TABLE OF CONTENTS

FOREWORD

This book is for every ordinary person to read and to discover how under God's leading they can do exploits for God.

I have been privileged to be Sue's prayer partner for the past 20 years and also her best friend. I have seen God accomplish the healing in her life that she writes about and also watched her come through into true freedom in God from all that held her in bondage. She is motivated entirely by God and the Holy Spirit, and always wants to see God get the glory in each and every situation. She has such a passion and love for Jesus because she has met Him personally and the one desire of her heart is that you meet Him too.

There is testimony after testimony in this book of the greatness of God and how He can break through into an ordinary life and accomplish His purposes.

Thelma Wilson
April 2010
Retired Co-Pastor, Highfield Community Church, Ashford, Kent

PROLOGUE

THE FINGER OF GOD

*But if I drive out demons by the finger of God, then
the Kingdom of God has come to you. Luke 11:20*

EARLY ONE MORNING IN 2000 I heard God speak to me: "I want you to teach on *'the finger of God'."* The passage of Scripture that came immediately to mind was in John 8 when the priests brought a woman, who had been caught in adultery, to Jesus and there are a few moments when Jesus simply writes in the dirt with His finger. Was He stuck for an answer? Was He playing for time? Had the priests outmanoeuvred Him? Was He doodling in the sand? NO, NO, NO. THIS WAS THE FINGER OF GOD WRITING IN THE DUST. We have no idea what He wrote...but one day when I meet Him in Glory I'm going to ask Him – because I'm curious!

Also came to mind were incidents last year – when during ministry and praying for someone, I felt led on a number of occasions to use my finger instead of laying on hands, with some surprising results. There were a couple of times when we, as a leadership team, were praying for a member in the body who had asked for ministry, and I could see, in the spirit, where the enemy was located. It was so clear, almost like 'X marks the spot', and God was saying: "Put your finger there."

This was so new to me, but I did – I put my finger on the spot. And each time I felt a reaction under my finger. On one occasion I flew over the pond to Northern Ireland to spend time with a friend who had cancer. When I laid hands on the tumour and prayed for her I could feel it moving under my hand.

"It's trying to get away!" I exclaimed, and we both broke into fits of laughter. Oh, how real the Joy of the Lord can be in the most difficult of circumstances. I knew that this cancer had a demonic source, and Satan was out to destroy this beautiful woman of God. But the more she suffered the more Jesus could be seen in her. Hallelujah!

Then, on another occasion when God told me to put *my finger* in the hole where a drain went into the centre of the cancer, the reaction was as though I'd put my finger into a light socket. Again I knew this was a demonic reaction to being touched by the anointing of God. By now I was way out of my depth but certainly on a learning curve with God, and I was an eager student. I was doing what He was telling me, and saying:

> "Lord teach me; show me what this is all about. Where are You leading me? I'm trusting in You, Jesus. Teach me more."

One Sunday morning our pastor Roy and his wife Margaret came into church. They were later than usual and he looked tired and was limping. We greeted each other with a hug, and I asked him if there was a problem. Yes, there was; he was in a lot of discomfort with phlebitis in his leg. It was serious; he'd had it before some years ago and had been hospitalised. He admitted he should have gone to the hospital the day before, but he decided to trust God, put prayer first and ask for ministry in church that morning.

We had a lovely time of worship – God had taught us well – that worship comes first in our lives; that He will bless it and the work that comes out of it. Roy then got up and explained his situation and asked if the whole church would gather round him and pray for him. Nobody needed asking twice! We sat him in a chair in the centre of the circle surrounding him, and he lifted up his trouser leg to reveal an inflamed, red patch on the front of his lower leg. It was hot to touch and in the centre was a hard lump. Whilst others were praying the Holy Spirit said to me: "Put your finger on the lump." I did so, gently, so as not to cause him any further pain. But there was an immediate reaction. I felt the lump move but didn't say anything. Then someone at the side of Roy shouted: "It's moving – I can see it!"

Roy was excited: "Wow! It's moving under your finger. I can clearly feel it."

I could feel it too. Recognising that this was an attack from the enemy, our corporate confidence in prayer grew and we rebuked the enemy and the spirit of infirmity in Jesus' Name. Immediately the lump visibly started to disappear for all to see, and the heat and swelling decreased. In a matter of minutes Roy could say: "I am healed. Praise God."

The next evening we had a leader's meeting. Roy turned up his usual cheerful self. When I enquired if his leg was okay, he teased me with a look of shock: "Sue, where is your faith?" He lifted up his trouser leg…not a mark! God had healed him and he never had any trouble with phlebitis again.

Roy went home to be with the Lord two years ago, and that is the total healing we all, as believers, look forward to. Heaven invites us to a party and Roy has already arrived to join in the celebrations.

Chapter 1

THE BEGINNING

*In the beginning God created the Heavens and
the earth. Genesis 1:1*

I **WAS BORN** on 10 May 1947 in St Woolos Hospital, Newport, Monmouthshire. I was a post-war baby, but although there was 'peace' in the world there was a certain amount of fear and trepidation in anticipation of my entry into the world. I was the second child to Herbert Moyce Chapman and Enid Sophia Chapman, nee Price. My sister – Christine Leonora – had arrived on July 5, 1938, very much a pre-war baby.

The deprivations of war...the rationing and the stress, had taken its toll on my mother's health, and she had spent ten months of 1945/6 in a TB (tuberculosis) isolation hospital. As my father worked long hours in the steelworks, my sister, Christine, had been looked after by Aunty Nell and Uncle Wally, my mother's sister and her husband, with their two children, Kate and Janet.

Not long after recovering from TB and returning home to pick up the reins of family life again, my mother discovered she was pregnant. She was still weak after such a debilitating illness, and really needed time to recuperate and get her strength back. So the joy that would normally accompany the news of a baby on the way was tinged with fear and concern for

1

my mother's life. To say that her doctor was so concerned that he advised her to have an abortion underlined the seriousness of the situation. Today, in 2010, with abortion virtually on demand, no one would have blinked an eyelid at such a suggestion; it's an everyday occurrence now for many lesser reasons. But in 1946 it was so different. As for the law, abortion was illegal. The only exception, as far as I am aware, was the real danger of the mother dying in childbirth.

And so my mother, recovering from the ravages of TB, was under pressure from a very concerned doctor – "You could die; you are not strong enough. I advise you to have an abortion."

But my mother's answer was a firm "NO".

It was against her conscience and religious beliefs as an Anglo-Catholic. Her mind was made up and she wasn't going to budge. My recollection of my mother was of a very fearful woman, so something greater than her fears motivated her at that time, for which I am eternally grateful. Otherwise I would never have been born; but I am so glad I was! So she went ahead with the pregnancy and the birth with the fear of death hanging over her. I never understood that at all until I was approaching middle-age myself; then I began to see…really see and understand for the first time, as I began to be healed and set free from my own lifetime of fears. That was a big crossroads for me.

But the first crossroads in my life was this very one that my mum was at. I was a six-week-old foetus in her womb, and she had a choice. Should she have this baby, or should she accept the doctor's plea for her to have an abortion? SHE CHOSE LIFE! She found it impossible to choose death and have the life inside her snuffed out. She instead chose *life*, even though she, herself, might die in the process, and the baby she was carrying also might die. As fearful as she was she could not bring herself to end my life in order to save her own. She chose *life*, and left the consequences to God. We *both* lived! And I am grateful to God and my mum for giving me life. It was no easy road for her by any means, and in the sixth month a miscarriage threatened and she spent the rest of her pregnancy pretty well as an anxious invalid.

But fortunately at full term I was born on that tenth day of May 1947. My mum later told me that it had been the worst winter ever, with snow on the ground from January till May 5 – just five days before my birth, and then summer arrived…as the comedian Tommy Cooper used to say – "jus' like that"! Of course I knew nothing of all that; I spent those cold months warm and snug inside. The accommodation was getting very cramped, but I didn't mind. I was preparing to enter the big wide world outside at just the right time!

Chapter 2

THE YEARS BETWEEN
TWO BIRTHS

*"I tell you the Truth," Jesus said, "no one can
enter the Kingdom of God unless he is born of
water and the Spirit. Flesh gives birth to flesh,
but the Spirit gives birth to spirit." John 3:5/6*

JESUS SAID, *"You must be born again." (John 3:7.)* He
was speaking to a man called Nicodemus, a Pharisee
genuinely interested in what Jesus had to say. Nicodemus was
totally confused, and questioned how a man could get back into
his mother's womb. Jesus questions him in *v.10: "You are
Israel's teacher and do not understand these things?"* The
expression 'Israel's teacher' or 'the teacher of Israel' indicated
that Jesus knew this man was the head of a rabbinic school, and
this experienced teacher would have been very familiar with the
expression 'to be born again'. In Pharisaic Judaism there were
six ways to be born again; they were all physical, and the last
way of being born again was to become the head of a rabbinic
school. This happened at about the age of fifty years, and so
Nicodemus would have used up all his opportunities to be born
again. Hence his genuine confusion at Jesus' imperative: *"You
must be born again."*

Large parts of the Christian church across the world are still
as confused as Nicodemus was, and have conjured up all sorts

4

of misinterpretations and doctrinal deviations to get over the problem, tragically leaving millions of people unaware that their eternal destiny is in grave danger. Jesus said it as simply as He could, but we do need the Holy Spirit, Who *is* the Spirit of Truth to open our eyes to *see* the Truth. When He said in *v.3: "I tell you the Truth, no one can see the Kingdom of God unless he is born again"*, He meant exactly what He said. And He was more than willing to stick in there with Nicodemus who genuinely wanted to grasp the things that Jesus was saying. So Jesus built on what He had already said using words that Nicodemus would understand. In *v.5* He speaks: *"I tell you the Truth, no one can enter the Kingdom of God unless he is born of water and the Spirit. Flesh gives birth to flesh, but the Spirit gives birth to spirit."*

Being born physically was given an expression by the Pharisees – 'being born of water'. Being born physically to a Jew was sufficient to enter the Kingdom of God. Therefore 'being born of water' was in the same way sufficient for a Jew to enter the Kingdom of God, for they are one and the same. Nicodemus believed this but was impressed by Jesus' teaching and was open to what He had to say, even though he felt a little uncomfortable because Jesus did not fit into the mould of Pharisaic Judaism.

But Jesus' teaching is clear – whether Jew or Gentile (that's me!) all must be born twice in order to enter the Kingdom of God…physical birth *and* spiritual birth.

I was born again, born of the Spirit of God, in September 1977, thirty years after I was born physically… born of water. Both were major crossroads in my life. There have been many crossroads since but these two births must rate as the most significant.

But what of the years between those two births – all thirty of them, from birth to the age which it appears, in the Bible, to be the point of maturity? Jesus Himself started His ministry at thirty years of age. When I was a teenager I saw the age of thirty as the first downhill step towards middle-age. Now, with my sixtieth birthday behind me I see thirty as stepping out of youth...just!

But a number of significant crossroads come immediately to mind as I think of those first thirty years. Passing the eleven-plus exam was seen as an achievement, and I was so pleased with myself. In 1958 I was aware, even in my tender years, that there was a stigma attached to failing this exam and having to go to a secondary modern school. The pressure, from my parents, to pass was quite considerable, particularly as my sister had passed and gone to a grammar school nine years before me, and was now at university. It was as though the future direction of one's life was determined by the result of this one exam. How important it was to my parents was clear, as they rewarded me with the one thing I had always longed for – a dog, a wire-haired fox terrier I called Mandy, my first pet. I was so happy!

At twelve years old I got into a school hockey team. Now that did have a big influence in the direction I was going to take in my life. Love of sport was in my genes, on my dad's side particularly. I can honestly say that sport became my god, and hockey was my first love, until, that is, I came face to face with a man called Jesus! Academically I had a love for languages and with it an ambition to get a degree in at least two languages, and become a court interpreter. But my hopes were dashed when my parents decided to move house. It was a good job move for my dad, and despite all my protestations the three of us moved to Romford in Essex in 1962. The change from the Oxford syllabus in Wales to the London syllabus in Essex brought real problems in my language studies. The courses were very different and I had left Wales halfway through my O-level studies. I had to work very hard and never really caught up on the coursework, but I did pass all the eight O-levels for which I sat. However, I had struggled and it had dented my confidence, and the passes in French and Latin weren't good enough for me to embark upon the ambitious career I had hoped for. I had no idea what to do next, and I stood at this particular crossroads for some time. I do believe that when I finally took a turning, it was the wrong one.

I was at a very high–achieving grammar school in Romford; as a result of a highly motivated headmistress…second best was *never* good enough. To my delight I started to excel in sport. I took part in everything and did really well; hockey still remained my first love, even though I did play county cricket for a few seasons. At the end of my second year I became School Games Captain, a position on equal standing with Head Girl in this particular school. Career-wise I was given the advice that if I loved sport so much then go to Physical Education College and train to be a PE teacher. I decided to take this advice. I succeeded, and in September 1965 I started a three-year course at Nonington College of Physical Education in Kent. I loved college life – the country house we lived in, the beautiful countryside it stood in, the community living, and the full-time sport. But by the time I was on my third teaching practice in my final year I was regretting the teaching bit. The college principal gave me her ear to get things off my chest, and persuaded me to give it a chance. I passed all my exams and set about looking for teaching vacancies in the 11–18 age groups.

This was no straight road…life rarely is. There are so many corners we cannot see around. Love has its way and I look back and see that God often has his way of surprising us just when we wouldn't have planned it! At the end of my second year at Nonington I met my future husband, Peter. He was Secretary of the Royal Cinque Ports Yacht Club in Dover and was invited to college social events. We were engaged after six weeks and married a year later, soon after leaving college. I had success in all my exams, and received my Teaching Certificate a few days later.

Married in Newport on August 3, 1968, Peter and I moved into a new house in Ashford, Kent, where Peter worked for a local bank, and I had acquired a position teaching in a local girls' secondary school. There were the good times at the school, but I really didn't enjoy teaching teenage girls, who but for a few exceptions, hated the sport I loved so much. It was soul destroying. I regretted having taken the advice that if I loved sport, then teach it. That was too simplistic. Coaching people who came to learn would have been a much better way of applying that advice. But I committed myself to the job with much encouragement from Peter and a very pastorally gifted headmistress.

Eighteen months later I was pregnant. Our first child, Ian Frederick, was born on January 6, 1971. What a miracle it is – to hold a newborn baby in your arms…unforgettable! And what a crossroads that was in both of our lives. We would never be the same again. I gladly gave up work and became a full-time mum. I even had to give up playing hockey because of a troublesome back injury collected in my last days at college. Just over three years later, on April 12, 1974, Christine Anne arrived on the scene, and our family was complete. I was twenty-seven years old. The next time I felt broody we got a puppy, our first dog, for the family!

Looking back from there I am sure the pre-school years are the most formative; both positive and negative input can get deeply rooted into the tender soul of early childhood. I believe it's an old Jesuit saying that goes something like: "Give me the child to the age of eight and I will show you the man."

My father's influence was very much to pass on his love of sport to me and the skills that make performing so enjoyable came from him. He applied the sporting principles of 'practice makes perfect', doing your best, aiming for the highest, being disciplined. Dad was a rugby fanatic – are not all the Welsh?! His International career was cruelly cut short at the age of sixteen when he twice broke the same leg during Welsh Trials. He was already seen as a brilliant winger and playing in the 'Probables'. From as far back as I can remember he was always teaching me different skills with a ball – handling, catching, kicking, and hitting skills. My sister had been given the same attention and both of us played hockey, and county cricket.

But I spent far more time with my mum and I see her as the greatest influence in my early life. In the forties and fifties most mums stayed at home and my mum was no exception. My dad went off to the steelworks before I was up in the morning, and until I was about six-years-old he came in after I had gone to bed.

I gradually became aware that my mother was not a very happy person, and the relationship between my mum and dad was far from right. Shouting at one another and arguing was normal for as long as I could remember. The verbal violence between them was really frightening at times, but the threat of actual physical violence was often close to the surface. It was not uncommon to see a carving knife glinting in the light as it was waved in the air with the threat that it would be used. Terrified, I would cry out: "Stop it, stop it!"

It was not a happy marriage. If there was any love and tenderness between them I cannot remember it, and I grew up in a home where there was anger and criticism, and yes, even hatred. How it got that way between them I do not know. But even though as a little child I never questioned that my mum and dad loved me, the home I grew up in was not a safe sanctuary of love and affection, and the seeds of insecurity and fear became embedded into my young life long before they began to bear fruit in my life and appear on the surface.

Two such fruit appeared by the age of twelve. The first was I developed a phobia; the second that I learned to bottle my emotions and not cry in front of anybody. Both had their roots in words spoken into my life in those early years by my mum. There was no way she was trying to damage me...she genuinely believed she was either protecting or disciplining me.

Chapter 3

FRUITS OF FEAR

The apostle John wrote: "There is no fear in Love. But perfect Love drives out fear, because fear has to do with punishment. The one who fears is not made perfect in Love." 1John 4:18

I LOOK BACK on my past and see 'a child of fear'. I was a happy person, but my sense of security was eggshell thin. Underneath the sunny exterior was a very insecure child, who grew into a very insecure adult. As soon as my relationship with God as Father began to develop, I found I could look back and have a deeper understanding of my mum. She was a very insecure and fearful person too who covered it the best way she could, with aggression, and a hard wall of self-protection. I never got to know her with this hindsight because she died when I was just twenty-one years old, and had only been married six months. But I did discover from a relative that as the youngest of ten children my mum grew up being made to feel that she was not planned, a bit of a mistake, and another mouth to feed. I believe mum inherited her own fears and insecurity as a result of being brought up in a large Victorian family, in an era when discipline was harsh, affection was seen as a weakness and 'children were seen and not heard', something I heard mum repeating many times! Her own mother, brought up under the same emotional repression, would have seemed severe rather than loving to her children, and with ten of them to bring up she wouldn't have had the time to give them personal love and affection, even if she knew how to. My mother in turn did not know how to love…to be tactile or to speak tenderly to us. She loved us in her own way, of that I am sure. But I believe she had a wounded spirit, and I in turn inherited that from her. I longed to be loved and cherished, but I didn't know how really to give love until God got hold of my life and started a deep and painful work of healing and deliverance. What a wonderful God I have!

The phobia I developed was a terror of vomiting, which I can trace back to the age of three. It was a warm sunny afternoon; mum washed my hair, and I couldn't wait to get back out into the garden to play. My dad was out there digging and he could usually be persuaded to play ball with me…he was sport mad! My mum's words followed me out:

"Stay in the shade, don't go in the sun…you will get sunstroke and be very sick." I played with my dad a bit, then sat in a deckchair for a while, and went indoors when mum called me for tea. She reinforced her words: "I hope you weren't in too much sun – you don't want to make yourself sick."

That night I woke up in the dark feeling very frightened. I didn't know what had happened, but it was horrible. I cried out, and it was my mum who came in to me and switched the light on. She was horrified. I had been sick in my sleep; my pillow was covered and it was all over my face and hair. Looking back, I realise that if I hadn't woken when I did I could have inhaled my own vomit and choked. I was acutely aware that my mother hated dealing with it, and gave me the "I told you so" admonition several times as she stripped my bed and cleaned me up in the bath. What I wanted most of all was a comforting hug to calm my fears and to assure me she still loved me. But she was coping in the best way she could with the situation, with her own fears showing, and that hug was not forthcoming. Even though the blankets were dried and aired thoroughly on the line the next day, the smell of vomit remained in them for a long time as a sober reminder that my mum was always right.

Six years later, at the age of nine, I came home from school with a request for a few extra pennies for dinner money that week because of the extra cost of a school Christmas dinner on the last day of term. My mum consented reluctantly with the words:

"Don't you eat pork if they give it to you. I don't expect they can afford chicken. But if they give you pork don't eat it or it will upset your tummy and make you sick." This brought back vivid memories of what it was like to be sick, but I had never been sick at all since that time when I was three. So off I went to school on the last day excited about the fun and games we had instead of 'proper' lessons, and looking forward to Christmas dinner.

When I got home my mum pounced on me: "What did you have for dinner? Did they give you pork? I hope you didn't eat it." I explained I had no idea what it was. It was just Christmas dinner and I enjoyed it. It was a slice of white meat, stuffing, roast potatoes, sprouts, carrots and gravy. And I ate it all...even the sprouts – not the favourite item of food for a nine-year-old. But my mum didn't share my joy: "If you are sick you can clean it up yourself; I told you not to eat pork."

By now I was becoming aware that she had a big problem with food herself, especially if eating away from home. Even at the home of her sister, my favourite aunt, mum warned me not to eat any of Aunt Ede's homemade cake because she kept it in a tin for such a long time it went stale and dry. From that time on I always disliked dry cake; it felt like it would get stuck in my throat, and I would choke. The seeds of a phobia now had deep roots and were about to manifest at the surface.

My aunt Ede and Uncle Billy moved to Weston-super-Mare. I had always loved visiting them from as young as I can remember. But I was developing a fear about mealtimes whenever I was away from home…even at my favourite aunt's. The simplest description I can give is of an irrational fear of choking when trying to swallow, and vomiting in the process and choking to death. At the age of twelve years mum and I were going for a week's holiday with Aunt Ede and Uncle Billy in Weston. I was looking forward to it. Dad was going to stay and look after Mandy, my dog. He was going to give us a lift to the train station. But as I got to the gate to get into the car I froze in absolute terror. I refused to go and I could not put into words why. Neither of them could budge me; I said I wasn't feeling well, so Mum went off to her sister's alone.

That phobia was now established, and surfaced throughout my teens and twenties whenever I felt in a vulnerable situation…basically – eating away from home. I met Peter in 1967 and the problem continued through a growing social life. I tried to fight it, and I tried to hide it, but to no avail. It had such a grip on my life. So I had to 'come clean' and tell Peter about it. He was very good about it, even though I don't know whether he understood it. Our children arrived when I was 24 and 27 years, and holidays were always a self-catering affair – usually caravanning. We all have enduring memories of some great holidays on St Tinney Farm in North Cornwall. And I was fine as long as we didn't go into a restaurant or café for a meal. I never talked to the children about it. What I had inherited from my mum I didn't want to pass on to them.

Brought up Anglo Catholic by my mum, (my dad claimed to be an atheist) I was christened at six-weeks-old and confirmed at eleven-years-old. But it wasn't until I was converted to Jesus Christ and born again spiritually that things began to change. Religion was transformed into a Relationship, and God took personal control of my life as I surrendered my life to Jesus. Various fears in my life gradually began to lose their grip or disappear completely as I prayed or had prayer and kept stepping out in faith. The last to go was the phobia about vomiting. I found there were times when I was freer from it than ever before, as my confidence in God grew. But then it would pop up and take me by surprise again. I cried out to God in desperation, and one day He gently challenged me: "We have thus far been chopping off branches of fear, and new ones are growing back because we haven't dealt with the root yet. If you will allow Me we can deal with the root together. Will you trust Me in this?"

I consented, with some trepidation, feeling that He was going to touch something so deep that *only His touch could reach it,* which meant me relinquishing complete control of my life to Him. And someone with fear in their life likes to be in control.

But I trusted Him, and in 1991 He delivered me dramatically from that phobia, and I have been completely free of it from that day. For me that was such a miracle and, as I write this, words from the hymn 'Amazing Grace' come to mind: 'my chains fell off, my heart was free; I rose, went forth and followed Thee.' Thank You my Heavenly Father!

So what about the second fruit? It appeared in my life as a result of the insecurity I felt as a child, in the atmosphere of the unhappy and sometimes violent marriage of my parents.

I gradually learned not to cry in front of anyone. I was, in myself, a happy child, born with an extrovert nature, full of fun and mischief! Even in the 1950s, with the ever-present threat of corporal punishment for my misdemeanours (both at school and at home), there was no quenching of my lively spirit! But I learned over a number of years not to cry in front of anyone. Why?

The pattern was set at home. 'Unconditional love' is a big 'grown-up' phrase, and as a child I couldn't put my desperate need into those terms. But looking back I see myself, as a child, needing just that. I feared rejection in the very place I should have felt most secure. It was a child's logic, but after my mum smacked me for being naughty, I didn't question the justice of it. I might have put my hands behind me and cried: "No mum, please don't," but I knew the punishment was inevitable. I would then run upstairs to my room, throw myself on my bed and sob my heart out. I look back and see this as normal. But so often my mum, hearing my crying, would shout up the stairs: "If you don't stop that noise I will give you something to really cry about."

What I longed for at that moment was her reassurance that, even though I had been naughty, she still loved me. All I needed was for her to come up and tell me so, and give me a cuddle just to make sure. But she never did that. So at first I would bury my head in my pillow to reduce the sound of my crying – I didn't want another smack. I just wanted to be loved; and I suppose taking into account the dysfunctional nature of my parents' relationship I often felt quite lonely at times…I was a child more acutely in need of reassurance and hugs than perhaps a child from a home where love was the pervading atmosphere of the home.

I developed other means for protecting what was so emotionally painful, determined not to be seen or heard crying, for *whatever* reason I happened to be doing so. I'd go and hide behind a tree at the top of the garden, or lock myself in the garage or garden shed. And when we moved house, to a village on the outskirts of Newport, when I was twelve-years-old, I would go across the road into the churchyard and not let the tears flow until I was on the far side of the church, facing the open fields.

As with the phobia, this carried on into my teens and twenties, married life and when I had children of my own. With them I certainly learned from my own experience, and after smacking them for being naughty (parents were still allowed to do so in the seventies and eighties), I would leave them for a short time and then go up to them to assure them I loved them, whether they were naughty or good, and I would give them a hug or a long cuddle – whatever was appropriate at the time. They were both different in their perceived needs; an arm around Ian's shoulder and a few words of reassurance, and he was up and gone. Christine needed the words of acceptance, but also the stillness of a prolonged cuddle. Being appropriate in one's behaviour towards offspring is a continual learning curve, and I feel at times that I still have parental 'L' plates on, and the children are now both in their thirties!

I was a quick learner as a new Christian, but sanctification is an ongoing, daily process, and deep inside me there was still something of a very insecure child, not sure at times that I was loved – an oversensitive adult, who prickled at perceived rejection, often reacting harshly to protect myself. I didn't like myself a lot of the time, which compounded the problem. And still I never let anyone see me crying, not even Peter, my husband.

Am I still the same now in 2010? NO, I have been healed of that wounded spirit!

But how?   Well, it was a long process…a wise God in control…His Holy Spirit accomplishing so much over fourteen years, and then a sudden breakthrough in 1991…

I will return to this, but I must go back to the moment in 1976 when out of the blue *'all things became possible.'*

Chapter 4

FIRST ENCOUNTER WITH THE LIVING GOD

If anybody does sin, we have one who speaks to the Father in our defence – Jesus Christ, the Righteous One. He is the atoning sacrifice for our sins, and not only for ours but also for the sins of the whole world. 1John 2:1/2

BORN AND BROUGHT UP in Newport, Mum took me to church from a very early age. Dad never went... he reckoned he was an atheist. I've always doubted that because he seemed to be afraid of God, but he blasphemed quite freely and 'for Christ's sake!' was his favourite expression. As a child I didn't like to hear him saying that, and mum took it as a personal insult. She was, in a way, deeply religious, but at the same time a deeply unhappy person. Her spiritual life was quite a mixture. Her church commitment was supplemented by fringe occult activity. She claimed to have ESP, dabbled in horoscopes, tealeaf reading, mind reading, and used a wine glass and letters of the alphabet to 'call up the spirits'. She often would speak of sensing an unseen presence, and when she said it was Jesus, even as a child I didn't feel comfortable with it.

Our church was Anglo-Catholic...very high, very ornate, lots of icons, statues, incense, bowing, making the sign of the cross, and bells ringing. I was christened as a baby...mum's choice, and confirmed at about eleven-years-old…sort of my choice with a bit of persuasion from mum and the curate that this was the right time to become a proper Christian. It was, in fact, another twenty years before I actually became a *real* Christian. At the time I didn't know that there was a difference between the religion I had practised from childhood, and the Relationship I discovered when I was thirty-years-old. It took God Himself to show me…

It was April 1976. My dad was living in Newquay and he had gone into hospital to have a routine operation. He had telephoned to say the op was delayed because blood tests showed he was anaemic. The next phone call was from Margaret, his landlady in Cornwall, saying she believed he had leukaemia, but the doctors wouldn't confide in her because she was not next of kin. Mum had died seven years previously, so that meant my sister and I were next of kin. Margaret urged us both to come down to Cornwall, to the hospital in Truro, to find out what exactly was going on with our dad.

My mind started to work overtime, imagining various scenarios, and I couldn't cope with any of them, including the phobia about eating away from home that consumed my thoughts. So I sat on the edge of my bed, in a quandary, and turned to God. Well, at least, I dug out of a drawer a little prayer book the Bishop had presented to me at my confirmation. I looked through it, reading out aloud the prayers that seemed vaguely appropriate. *None of them* actually said what I really wanted to say. So I closed the book, put it down, lifted my head and prayed what I *now* realise was the first prayer I had ever really prayed from the heart – "God, I've believed in you all my life. *If* you are real – HELP ME – I can't cope with all this."

So Chris and I drove down to Cornwall that weekend leaving husbands Peter and Philip in charge of the five children! We visited dad and Chris had a word with the doctors and he did have leukaemia, acute myeloid leukaemia. At my dad's age (sixty-six years) they were not very optimistic about the outcome of the treatment. Prognosis? They were not sure – months probably, possibly a year at the most. Dad didn't know and we didn't tell him at that stage, which made the visit very stressful for us. We didn't want to tell him such distressing news and then disappear off home, 300 miles away. We visited him briefly again on the Sunday morning before starting the long drive back to Sussex. We weren't to know that this was to be the last time we'd see him. He rang us in the evening to see if we had got back safely and to tell us he'd had a very mild stroke, the effects of which were already wearing off.

Three days later we had a phone call from the sister-in-charge of the ward informing us that he'd had another stroke. We asked whether it was urgent enough to come down to visit him. She said that if we'd lived closer then the answer would be 'No', but living so far away we may feel happier in doing so. This time Chris and Philip went off to Cornwall, leaving their children with us. I remember it so well that after they drove off Peter gathered all five children and myself together around him on the driveway, explaining to us all what was going on, and suggesting we all say the Lord's Prayer together, *for Granddad* – a most poignant memory.

Our day went well – having five young children around took all our time and energy, and was a great distraction from worrying! Peter went off to evening classes after tea – Coastal Navigation was the course this particular term. I eventually got all the children off to bed and went up to have a bath just as the BBC Nine O'clock News was about to begin. It was to be a quick bath as there was something on the telly at 9.25 p.m. that I wanted to watch!

As I stepped into the bath *something happened*...something that was going to change my life for ever. I had one foot in, and one foot out, and I was suddenly overcome by a tremendous sense of darkness, cold, and what felt like a heavy ice-cold stone resting in my heart. I shuddered. I seemed to know instinctively that it was my dad…that he was dying. I quickly got into the bath hoping the warmth of the water would take away the coldness. It didn't. I felt an inexplicable urgency to pray for my dad. Apart from the set prayers in church this was not something I did. The urge to do so seemed to be coming from outside of myself. So I opened my mouth, and what a surprise I got when the first stumbling words turned into a torrent of prayer…words coming out of my mouth faster than I could think of them. Most of it was so fast I cannot recall it – but I do remember pleading with God to forgive my dad, and to save him. (At that time I knew very little of what *that* meant!) As I continued to pray, at a momentum that was not my own, I had a picture. It was of a hedge in winter…a thick, very prickly hedge with very little foliage on it. All the time I prayed it was as though I had hold of one end of my dad and someone else the other side of the hedge held the other end of him; and we were in a tug-of-war for my dad, pulling him back and forth through this prickly hedge. I felt strongly that it was a matter of life and death, though I didn't understand why. But I wasn't going to let go. How long I prayed I don't know. It was as though time stopped still, but as I prayed, hardly taking time to breathe, I was utterly amazed to hear myself. I had never prayed like this before. Where was it all coming from?

Then, suddenly, all was still.

The heaviness, the coldness and darkness lifted and in an instant was replaced by such a warmth and peace, a lightness in my heart, and a sense of being bathed in light...the sun had come out in my bathroom in the middle of the night, and was shining on me and warming me up!

I knew, with a knowing that can *never* be taken from me, that I had just encountered God – and it was He Who had helped me pray for my dad who was dying. I also knew that my dad had *just* died, but that he was all right. I spoke out aloud:

"THAT'S GOD! AND MY DAD'S OKAY. THANK YOU GOD, THANK YOU."

A peace continued to sweep over me, a peace like I'd never known before. I stood up in the bath and stepped out. I heard the theme music for the end of the evening news. It was 9.25 p.m. My dad must have died between 9.15 p.m. and 9.25 p.m., of that I was certain. But it was all okay. I dried myself and got dressed and made my way slowly downstairs, wondering how I was going to tell Peter all of this. By the time he got home from his evening classes at 9.45 p.m. I couldn't bring myself to say anything...it was too precious. What on earth would he think? I didn't want to be misunderstood, and I didn't want to upset him. I kept it in my heart and waited...

No more than ten minutes later there was a knock at the door. It was Peggy, a neighbour from just over the road. We didn't have our own telephone and she kindly let us use hers for urgent calls. There was a phone call from Chris and Philip, from the hospital in Cornwall. Peter hurried over to Peggy's, leaving me to ponder...and wait...*knowing*....

Peter returned five minutes later. He walked slowly into the kitchen, looking at me, *and I knew*. I helped him out: "It's my dad, isn't it?"

"Yes," he replied.

"My dad has died, hasn't he?"

For a moment he gave me a curious look, and then confirmed what I already knew. He wrapped his arms around me in a big warm hug and started to give me some of the details. But I had *only* one question – "What time…what time did he die?"

He died round about 9.20 p.m. I felt a tingle of joy in my heart at that confirmation.

Apparently Chris and Philip, having driven through horrendous thunderstorms and torrential rain, had arrived just a few minutes too late. They never saw him before he died to say goodbye. I felt *so* sorry for them. But for myself, I had a tremendous peace and a settled feeling that remained constant and never wavered as the truth sunk in and we had to get on with preparations for the funeral. I felt secure, very still deep inside, and at peace with the whole situation. Grief had no power in all this for me. My dad was okay.

God had taken me totally by surprise…I never realised He could be *that* real, but that first encounter with the Living God brought me to a brand new crossroads, and unknown to me I was being led by the Spirit of God, from that moment, down a straight path, without detours, to a Cross.

Chapter 5

JOURNEY INTO LIFE

*Jesus said: "I tell you the Truth, I am the gate;
whoever enters through Me will be saved. He
will come in and go out and find pasture… I have
come that you may have life, and have it to the
full." John10:7-10*

IT WAS EIGHTEEN MONTHS later, on September 8, 1977, that I accepted Jesus Christ as my Lord and Saviour. I had not realised until then, that from that first encounter with a *real* God, He had His hand on my life and had never let go of me. The night my dad died I may have lost my earthly father, but I discovered that I had found my Heavenly Father…or He had found me, and wasn't His timing perfect! But, of course, I didn't understand all this in the beginning, because *'Faith comes by hearing the message, and the message is heard by the Word of Christ.' Romans 10:17*.

I started going to church occasionally, then more regularly – perhaps once a month, then fortnightly, and after about a year I was going most Sundays. I read my Bible occasionally, with no idea where to start…but the beginning. I was looking for Truth, but starting at Genesis 1 was a tough place for me to start. I already had a fixed mindset about the beginning of the Bible because I had been taught at school that the early stories in the Bible, including the creation story, were myths. So armed with pen and paper I opened my old school Bible, with a critical attitude. I wrote down questions when I was curious but didn't understand, and I wrote down what I thought were obvious contradictions. One verse that struck me more than any other was God's command to Adam:

> *'You are free to eat from any tree in the garden; but you must not eat from the tree of knowledge. If you eat of that you will surely die the same day.' Genesis 2:16/17.*

Adam *did* eat the fruit, disobeying God, *but he didn't die the same day,* did he? So what does that mean? I had no idea; I was totally in the dark. 'It's a contradiction; it must be an error,' I wrote in my notes.

Months later, after I was converted, the Holy Spirit was now my teacher and He took me back to the beginning of the Bible and shone His Light on that verse. It was as though scales fell from my eyes, and I understood immediately that Adam *did* die the day that he disobeyed God's command…yes he lived on physically, but *that* day he died spiritually, his relationship with God destroyed by his sin.

How amazing! 'Once I was blind, now I could see!' From that moment I started an adventure in the Word of God, with the Holy Spirit as my teacher, and over thirty years on as I write this, it is still an exciting adventure!

So from that first encounter with God, the Holy Spirit was on my case…the Spirit of Truth drawing me to the Truth, and inevitably He pointed me to Jesus, and the night when I understood that Jesus had died on the Cross to reconcile sinners (like me) to God…then I suddenly realised it was not just 'God' I'd met that night. It was Jesus.

He said: *'No one can come to the Father except through Me.' John 14:6.* I had met the Saviour and I knew that He loved me and wanted to save me. I learned that Jesus is the Mediator between me and God, and seated at God's right hand He is ever interceding on my behalf. The memory of the night when my dad died flashed back. I'd prayed like I'd never known how to pray. God was helping me pray for my dad. It was Jesus – interceding on my dad's behalf with me. And what was the tug-of-war through the hedge? It was the devil, surprised by the sudden change of circumstances, fighting for his rights to my dad's life. After all, hadn't my dad happily lived under his domain for years? The tug-of-war had been for my dad's eternity. And I began to realise it had been for my eternity too.

I learned a valuable lesson for the future from my dad's last minutes on earth. God can meet a man on his deathbed, and no one else may know, and no one can judge what goes on in those twilight moments before a man breathes his last breath. *'But many who are first shall be last, and the last first.' Matthew 19:30 (NKJ)*

I believe, because of the nature of my experience with God that night, that my dad met Jesus before he died, and made the right choice, probably with his dying breath. But I must let God be God – and leave the mystery of it all to be revealed in His good and perfect time. I am sure there are going to be a number of surprise meetings in Glory!

Oh, how much God must love me! This was new to me – something I could hardly cope with. And in the final few weeks before my conversion I had an increasing experience of the Love of Jesus – time and again overwhelmed by ocean waves of love rolling over me and bringing me to my knees, in tears, and my heart bursting with love and joy in response.

Clouds of apprehension occasionally cast a shadow over the sun and its warmth (spiritually, that is). What if I lose this? How can I keep it? This is so precious to me. It is so new to me, but I *never* want to lose this wonderful sense of the presence of Jesus, and the overwhelming power of His Love.

I talked to God about it: "What do I do, God? I'm already a mature Christian, aren't I? I'm confirmed, and I have been taking Communion since I was eleven years old. What else is there to do? I don't want to lose You." This I prayed lunchtime one day at the beginning of September 1977. I was in the midst of preparing lunch…Peter would be in any moment. Pinafore on and fish slice in hand, I sank to my knees, tears pouring down my face, as I was yet again overwhelmed by waves of Divine Love.

An hour later I had just waved Peter goodbye and there was a knock at the kitchen door. There stood Rev. Christopher Woods, my minister. He simply said: "Sue, are you ready to commit your whole life to Jesus Christ?"

Revelation hit me – I've never done that…*that's* what I must do.

"Yes, I am ready," was my reply.

"Then go and pray," he said. With that he turned and left. I was suddenly overwhelmed with gratitude, so grateful to God for sending this man….so grateful to Christopher for coming. Even though I had not breathed a word to anyone concerning what had happened to me over the past eighteen months, Chris had actually recognised the signs…the signs of God working in my life, and the Holy Spirit drawing me closer to Jesus. And he had picked just the right moment to knock on my door. I knew from that brief encounter that he understood, that he'd noticed something special going on in my life, and he knew what it was! I was so grateful; it simply authenticated all that I'd been through.   It was true, and someone else knew as well, and understood.

I went straight upstairs....there was no reason to delay. I sat on the edge of my bed and prayed a very simple prayer: "Lord Jesus, I know I've made a real mess of my life up to now. I just want You to come in and take control. I hand over the reins of my life to You now. I no longer want to be in control. I want You to come in and run my life from this day forward."

No flashing lights or voices from Heaven; just a solid deep down certainty that He was no longer on the outside but on the inside. *Now* I felt His Presence and Love were safe. I'd never lose them. He'd answered my lunchtime prayer of just over an hour before. I felt I'd reached a journey's end, and had stopped travelling and was still, at rest, and at peace...and oh what PEACE! I knew that what I had just done was not only my desire, but also His desire, and He had got me there...and *it was PERMANENT*.

But it was just the beginning...I had been born again. And I was on a 'Journey into Life.'

Chapter 6

POWER TO WITNESS

*But you will receive power when the Holy Spirit
comes on you; and you will be my witnesses in
Jerusalem, and in all Judea and Samaria, and to
the ends of the earth. Acts 1:8*

DURING THE SUMMER of 1977 Youth with a Mission
were in town for six weeks. Their logo – 'TURN THE
TOWN' – and Ashford was the town that was to be
turned…back to God. Otherwise known as YWAM, they were,
and still are, an international evangelistic Christian mission.
Even as a very new Christian it didn't take me long to
understand a popular statement I often heard on the lips of other
believers – "There are no coincidences with God, just God-
incidences." My conversion on September 8 that year had me
beginning to look at *everything* with new eyes and seeing God
in it all. No matter how major or mundane something was He
was always there…always involved, and things often just fell
into place…just the right thing at the right time. I was amazed;
I was excited. This was *some* journey I was on…what an
adventure!

Two days after my conversion Christopher Woods took me
to the evening meeting of Turn the Town in the big top erected
in Victoria Park the other side of Ashford. Wow, I'd never
been to anything like this before! My irregular church-going

Anglican experience had never even stretched to attending a Bible Study, and I wouldn't have known what to do with a prayer meeting! This was a totally new experience for me. But my spirit within me was profoundly moved and encountered God afresh as the gathering moved through worship and praise, prayer, and testimony. Strange and new as it was, I felt as though I had arrived home after a long search, and the God I was meeting here, in this big tent, was the same God I met for the first time the night my dad died eighteen months earlier, and the same God of Love Who had been pursuing me so passionately in recent weeks. Everything I had experienced in the solitude, alone with Him, I was now experiencing in the midst of hundreds of worshipping believers. I had never shared a word with anyone about my 'God experiences' for eighteen months, and now I was sharing in a corporate experience the *same* fellowship with the *same* God, and the *same* Love and Peace and Joy and the *same* Life, as I had from that very first encounter. This was *no* coincidence; I got the feeling that God had planned it this way. I may have had no idea what He was up to, but *He* knew, and my love for Him grew that evening.

The message was brought by a young minister who gave a personal testimony of how he had realised that accepting Jesus Christ as his Saviour was not enough to go out and preach the Gospel and do the will of God. He read from Acts 1 and 2 and then told this story: "When I was at theological college I prayed and asked God for the gift of tongues, after hearing my tutor teaching on Acts 1 and 2. I prayed a number of times becoming increasingly desperate. But *nothing* happened. So I went to my tutor and said:

"'I have asked and received nothing.'

"'What have you been asking for?' my tutor asked.

"'The gift of speaking in tongues, just as the disciples received at Pentecost,' I replied.

"'You are asking for the wrong thing,' said my tutor.

"Baffled I enquired: 'What should I be asking for then?'

"'Look at Acts 1:8 again, John. Read it and tell me what Jesus promised his disciples when the Holy Spirit came upon them and they received the baptism with the Holy Spirit. What were they to receive?'

"'*POWER*...it says *power!*'

"'Power for what?'

"'Power to witness."

"'John, you need to be praying the right prayer. You've been praying for the gift of tongues because you've heard other students speaking in tongues. Yes?'

"'YES,' I replied.

"'Well, go back to your room and start asking God for *power to witness* for Jesus in this world wherever He sends you. That's what you want...that's what you are here for John, isn't it?'

"'Yes, yes it is!'

"'Then ask Jesus to baptise you in the Holy Spirit and give you power to witness for Him. And come back and tell me how you get on.'"

And John told us: "I went back to my room and got down on my knees and did just as my tutor had directed me. And ...wow! The Holy Spirit just came down upon me, and something started to well up within me at the same time...and it kept coming, till it spilled out of my mouth. Jesus said: '*Streams of Living Water will flow from your hearts...*' and '*....out of the mouth the heart overflows!*'

"That's what it felt like, and what came out of my mouth were words I couldn't understand, but my spirit within me was jumping for joy!

"Now I understood that at first I had been praying from the wrong end – praying for the overflow *before* asking for the filling. Now I was experiencing tongues *as* the overflow, and the evidence of being *filled to overflowing*. I left my room with a new boldness and great joy, witnessing to everyone I met on the way. I eventually arrived at my tutor's office, and he took one look at my face and said with a smile: 'Prayer answered then?'"

The invitation to come forward was made to all those who wanted power to witness for Jesus. I was on the edge of my seat ready to move. That's just what I needed. Fear had kept me from telling even my husband about what God had been doing in my life, and about my conversion. I knew that this power to witness was my greatest need at this moment. But before anyone could move a sobering condition was added. Only those who were ready to surrender their lives to the Lordship of Jesus Christ, and be willing to go anywhere in the world He might choose to send them…even Russia. The word 'Russia' was enough to stop anyone in their tracks, and certainly a cold chill went down my spine. But the desire to 'go' for God and be a witness for Jesus was, at that moment, greater than any mention of Russia, still, in the seventies, in the deep darkness of communism. I committed myself and my family to God. He knew my heart and He knew all about my husband and two young children. I didn't want to go to Russia, but if He wanted to send me there, I was willing. I made my way down from the back of the tent and joined the growing line in front of the stage.

It seemed that I was standing there for ages. I felt a little self conscious at first... I had *never* done anything like this before. But I closed my eyes and began to relax as the worship continued. I felt part of it, and there was that Peace again settling deep inside me.

A light touch on my shoulder and someone spoke: "Would you like me to pray with you?" I turned and looked into the face of a black African. It was Julius…he had been introduced earlier. He and his wife, Margaret, had come over from Nigeria at the invitation of YWAM, to minister during that particular week of the Mission.

"Yes," I whispered, in answer to his question.

He asked me what I wanted God to do for me, and I shared my story and told him why I had come out. He led me in prayer; I thanked God for all that He had done in my life and I asked Him to deal with any fears that prevented me opening my mouth for Him. And would He fill me with His Spirit, and give me the power and the courage to open my mouth and witness for Him wherever He sent me. What amazed me is that I started praying quietly, and got louder, and by the end I could actually hear myself shouting out to God!

When we had finished praying Julius said: "Now pray and thank God, thank Him fifty times…never stop thanking Him for what He has done for you tonight."

My silent reaction to that was that I didn't feel any different at that point, and I opened my eyes and turned to Julius to say that to him. As I looked into his eyes I was amazed – this guy was *sure* that God had done something, and in that moment I trusted him rather than my own feelings. In retrospect I realise that, in that look, his faith ignited my faith. Didn't Jesus sometimes say to someone seeking healing: "Look at Me?"

And one look into His eyes stirred up the faith in them that was in Him, and they received.

So I closed my eyes again to pray, and started to thank Him – just simply that. I felt Julius quietly move away, as I repeated the words: "Thank you Lord…thank you Lord." And as I did this I felt a great surging sensation inside of me…excitement and great joy. Words are inadequate to describe it. And God supplied my need, as He does! For as this was happening I kept on praying…I knew I must keep on praying. More than anything I *wanted* to keep on praying! And all I was praying was: "Thank you Lord, thank you Lord…" And one word ran into the next, and within seconds I was no longer saying "Thank you Lord". I didn't understand *what* I was praying – it was fast and fluent and very real.

Then the realisation of what was happening hit me. God was answering my prayer. The Holy Spirit was all over me *and* inside me. I was opening my mouth and witnessing to the Lord in prayer in a way I never imagined was possible…such power! Someone going past me stopped and listened and praised the Lord. It was Julius' voice.

When I stopped praying, I just stood there, drinking it all in. I felt an overwhelming Love for God, but not for Him alone. I felt the same Love for everyone in that tent, a love for people that I had never experienced before. I became aware that my hands were reaching to the heavens – very un-Anglican maybe, but very natural for the new 'me' that God was creating at yet another of His crossroads. I also became aware of everyone singing: "I love you with the Love of the Lord," and I realised this was the Love of Jesus welling up within me, and it wasn't for keeping to myself. It was for sharing – for giving away.

Chapter 7

COME TO THE CROSS

The next day John saw Jesus coming towards him
and said:
"Look, the Lamb of God, who takes away the sin
of the world." John 1:29

IWAS JUST A TODDLER in Christ, less than three years
old spiritually, when one day God spoke to me the words
above – "Come to the Cross." I had a basic knowledge of the
meaning of the Cross – that Jesus was the Son of God who had
come down from Heaven; lived the life of a good man on earth;
at the age of thirty-three was crucified, He died and was buried;
and the third day He rose again from the dead. These words I
had been familiar with since childhood, for we recited them in
the liturgy at every communion service, and Easter was the
most important event in the church calendar.

But any deeper understanding was not as yet in my grasp. I
simply accepted it all by faith, and didn't realise that God was
just about to grow my faith, *and* my understanding, *and* my
love for Him.

It was a Sunday evening in March 1980. Peter had gone
alone to the evening service at church. Usually we went
together, but there was within me an indefinable restlessness,
and so I decided to take a rain check on corporate worship and

spend some time alone in a quiet time with God. I settled down on the floor in front of the fire to have a time of prayer. Within seconds God spoke to me –

> *"Come to the Cross...*
> *...stay at the Cross.*
> *Look at the Cross, and keep looking at Jesus on the Cross."*

He then started to show me where I'd recently been in my Christian walk.

I'd come to the Cross, back to the Cross, time and time again. I'd come and asked for, and received and thanked the Lord for forgiveness of my sins. I'd come to the Cross realising it is the only place to receive forgiveness. That's the place where Jesus had died for my sins, paid the wages, and received forgiveness for me.

I'd stayed at the foot of the Cross for cleansing. *"The Blood of Christ cleanses us from every known sin,"* the Bible says. I'd come for washing. I'd had to come closer for that – to be washed in the Blood. Perhaps I'd always wanted to stay my distance and not see *too* clearly. But to be washed in the Blood I'd needed to get as close as I could, and I'd seen so much more. I'd seen the feet and the wounds and the nails and the Blood.

Once cleansed I'd asked for a new infilling of the Holy Spirit, and then I'd turned and gone on my way to get on working for the Lord.

The Lord had me face what I'd been doing, and what to do next. Yes, I'd been coming to the Cross; yes, I'd been looking and seeing Jesus hanging there; yes, I'd known forgiveness, cleansing and filling; and yes, I *turned* away and went about my business – to return another day.

The Lord was saying a new thing – "Don't keep returning – *STAY – at the Cross.*" How did He bring this home to me? He spoke to me as soon as I started praying –

> *"I am the Good Shepherd, and I am ready to die for my sheep."*

I looked at Jesus on the Cross, and there He was, the Good Shepherd dying for His sheep. And *I* was one of those sheep looking on.

> *"All of us are like lost sheep each going his own way."*
> *Isaiah 53:6*

I was not a member of an exclusive fold. He didn't just go out looking for one lost sheep in a hundred. Every last member of the human race is a lost sheep, and He died for them all, and He seeks each one.

> *"For God so loved the world that He gave His one and only Son, that* whosoever *believes in Him shall not perish but have Eternal Life."*
>
> > Jesus' own words in *John 3:16*.

And so He hung there – my Shepherd, dying for me because I'd got myself lost. I was at that moment just grateful that I recognised Him; I knew His voice; *I felt safe.*

Not just the Shepherd – dying in order to save me.

But there was also the Lamb – dying in *my* place.

"Keep looking, Sue..."

There hung – the Saviour
Also – the Sacrifice.

I wanted to look away and pray about something else, but I knew He was revealing to me what I needed to know, needed to admit, and needed to ponder on.

Again, dying there – the Son of God... God Himself.
And – the Son of Man… a man, innocent of any crime.

The horror of the Cross and what happened that day began to sink in, at this time, in a new way. The Lord was gently bringing me to the point of facing up to a few home truths, maybe stuff that I'd tucked away because it made me feel uncomfortable. Several times I'd wanted to look away… get on and pray about something else. But I recognised His gentle leading – "Keep looking and you'll see the Truth. I can only show you the Truth if you keep your eyes fixed on *Him*."

So I kept looking, but I'd been this way before. He took me back to my childhood. We had the Stations of the Cross all around the church, framed in relief form – ivory figures on a sky blue background. Often when my mum was busy chatting after the service or doing the church flowers, I would wander around again and again just to look at them. I was fascinated but at the same time horrified at the graphic portrayal of the physical suffering Jesus must have gone through. Time and again I recoiled and looked away. I didn't want to think about it any more… until the next time. Oh, the curiosity of innocence!

Now, all those years later, at the age of thirty-two, God was speaking to me: "Look at the Cross, and *keep* looking." And this time I was still going through the same reaction, but I kept looking. He drew me closer in and I looked. I realised that up to this time I'd stood back and looked, and got a general impression from a distance. I realised that this was self-defence. I'd never been prepared for the consequences of a closer look.

What did I see? This was my vision – the one God gave to me when I joined the Greeks in their cry when they approached the disciples: "We would see Jesus!" Now it was clearer than it had ever been. It stood out; it was real; there was no fuzziness about this. *ONE VISION - JESUS - JESUS ON THE CROSS.* This is the vision, never to lose sight of until that day I see Him in all His Glory.

> *NOW – Hanging* on the Cross – Judged for me.
> *THEN –* In Glory – as Judge.
> *VISION – JESUS – THE TRUTH – LOVE*

This had been my vision of late, and it was all there – on the Cross – complete.

What did I see? *JESUS.* I averted my eyes as a child because of the horror of the physical torture. That was still there. But now there was much more. I had been turning away since my conversion for another reason – *I LOVE HIM.* If I didn't look too closely…if I misted up the picture a bit…if I kept the event firmly in the past…then it wouldn't hurt so much. But it did because He means so much to me, and I love Him. So He said: "Keep looking, don't look away now."

So I looked, and only in looking did I then discover, in a way that I'd never known before that – *I AM FORGIVEN.*

What did I see? *THE TRUTH.* I saw the sheer frailty of human flesh. I saw details of physical suffering taking the human frame beyond the point of endurance, to death. Dirt, sweat, and blood running down His body; muscles tearing;

wounds gaping; a bulging ribcage struggling to move up to delay suffocation; I saw His head, the only part of His body able to move, lolling occasionally from exhaustion, but more often looking and leaning towards the people – the only gesture He could make towards those He loved. I looked and I realised that even in my meanest of moments in the past I would never have wished *that* on any man, not the lowest of criminals…NO ONE.

And yet there hung Jesus – a man without sin, but more – God Himself – and I had helped to put Him there…and *He loved me!* I couldn't take that in. I just accepted it. I felt deep gratitude again – as I have done ever since.

God is Love. When I look at Jesus, what do I see? *LOVE*, again and again. I look now at Jesus on the Cross and what do I see? *LOVE*…Love that I cannot comprehend – 'the greatest act of Love the world has ever known.' I know without a doubt that it is directed at me. I just want to respond. I don't now even ask how. I'll just stay at the Cross; I'll keep my eyes on Jesus, and I'll respond to others at the same time as I am gazing at Him. Jesus is the answer. He is every answer. A new friend recently said: "Jesus is the answer. What's the question?!"

So any answer I need I'll leave to Him. I'm just going to stay where He has brought me. Then I won't get in the way of whatever He wants to do through me.

A few days later I read Jesus' words in *John's Gospel:*

> *"He that hath seen me has seen the Father."*
> *"The words that I have spoken do not come from Me. The Father Who remains in Me does His own work."*
> *"I and the Father are one."*
> *"The Father remains in Me."*

How long did the Father remain in Jesus?

The Father remained in the Son all the way through the suffering, the torture, the ridicule. The Father remained in the Son as He was laid on the rough Cross and the nails were driven home. The Father remained in the Son as the Cross was lifted up and the hands and feet took the full weight of the body. The Father suffered with the Son.

Then the sins of the whole world rained down upon Him, and poured into His ever-open heart. A Holy God cannot look upon sin. As His Son became filled with sin, sin that was ours, not His own – the Father had to do the only thing a Holy and Just God could do – *LEAVE – TURN AWAY.*

"My God, my God, why have You forsaken Me?"

That is the price of sin – separation from God, the severing of the most precious of relationships – between God and man – *HELL*. Jesus was left utterly alone – a man dying a terrible death…without God…the time he'd need God most of all.

He did it for us. He did it for me.

It was an expression of Man's worst deed versus God's best Love.

It's a week later. I'm still at the Cross. He's told me to stay and that's where He is teaching me so much. That's where I see the Truth. One thing is clearer – I *need* to stay there, close to Him, allowing Him to bear the burden of my sin. How foolish it would be if I were to creep away under the weight of a particular sin, to sink down against the walls of Jerusalem, at a distance from Calvary, and try and sort it out for myself. It's no good me suffering there when a hundred yards away the Lamb of God is suffering in my place. I need to stay as close as I can to the Cross and let Him take the burden. I asked a friend who had known the Saviour longer than I: "How close to the Cross can I get?"

Her reply: "On it."

> *I HAVE BEEN CRUCIFIED WITH CHRIST. IT'S NO LONGER I THAT LIVETH BUT CHRIST WHO LIVETH IN ME. I LIVE THIS LIFE NOW, IN THE FLESH, BY FAITH IN THE SON OF GOD, WHO LOVED ME AND GAVE HIMSELF FOR ME.*
>
> *Galatians 2:20 KJV*

Chapter 8

MY BAPTISMAL JOURNEY

Repent and be baptized, every one of you, in the Name of Jesus Christ for the forgiveness of your sins. Acts 2:38

TO BE OR NOT TO BE BAPTIZED – that is the question, and what a question, what a *tricky* question. This subject has divided Christendom down the ages, and many saints have died for this part of their faith's profession. I have been, up to now, reluctant to include this part of my Christian experience in this book for fear of misunderstanding, causing offence…even stirring up anger from the more extreme theological pugilists.

But out of the blue God put His finger on *this* crossroads in my life and simply said: "Now is the time. Do it now, Sue." He then brought to mind Jane, my first Christian friend and prayer partner, who said to me when I was a mere babe in Christ: "Sue, listen to me. You have a ministry for being misunderstood. People won't understand God's calling on your life. But don't worry about them. Trust *Him*. He understands, and He will *never* let you down. Just keep on obeying Him." (Jane High, 1979.)

And so I am reminded that this is an autobiography…a very personal story, and I will tell it like it was, and is. To do otherwise would be dishonest and not honourable to my Heavenly Father.

1977 – I was converted to Jesus Christ and baptized in the Holy Spirit, with tongues. I had a sudden and brief revelation of the relevancy of water baptism there and then. But I dismissed it just as quickly, as unnecessary, as I had been 'done' as a baby.

1978 – After a year with the Holy Spirit as my teacher and the Bible as my textbook, I had no doubt that the Scriptures taught baptism by immersion of those already believers, who had repented toward God and put their faith in Jesus Christ…that baptism was a command, the first command to the new believer. I wanted to be obedient…I needed to be obedient to God.

So I went to my minister and asked for believer's baptism. What a predicament I put him in! He'd seen the work of the Holy Spirit bringing me to conversion, and he'd been with me when I was baptized in the Holy Spirit. On a personal level He felt very close to me and very involved in my spiritual walk. But theologically he had a big problem – I had been 'baptized' as an infant. I asked him to explain to me the Church of England theology on baptism because I saw confusion between Paul's statement in Romans that *"Baptism is burial,"* and the fact therefore that I'd been *buried* as an infant thirty years before I had *died* to sin.

I knew he had registered what I was saying, but as a priest he had to abide by the official line. And he pointed out that in the view of the church the practice of infant baptism was the New Covenant alternative to Jewish Circumcision. It was something to do with bringing your child into the covenant family of God – the Jew by circumcision, the Christian by infant baptism. Even in my present state of Christian infancy I knew that there was no way that Scripture taught that sprinkling water on a baby's head could make the child born again spiritually. It seemed that this involved some superstition. Clearly Scripture taught – born again *first…then* baptism. I asked him for a Scripture to 'prove' infant baptism. He gave me one: Acts 16:25-34 – the account of Paul and Silas in jail, the earthquake, the conversion of the jailer, who took them home at midnight and the Gospel being preached to the whole household, who believed and were baptized immediately. My minister said there must have been babies in that household, so that they must have baptized the babies as well. I commented that it seemed that they were deliberately putting babies there just to support a man-made doctrine; also, if the true teaching of baptism was followed (hear the Gospel, believe, repent and be baptized), then babies would have been left asleep in their cribs, whilst those that were old enough to hear and understand, would have been rejoicing in their new found faith.

Needless to say he felt he had to refuse my request for believer's baptism, and I sympathised with his reasons. I went back to God. What shall I do, Lord? I just want to obey you.

Two months later I went to a baptism service at the Baptist church in the centre of town – to watch, not to be baptized, although I would have been prepared to get wet if a call to anyone had been made. But that wasn't to be. I continued to seek God:

"I suppose I'll have to go up the road to our local Baptist church when the time is right? You tell me when. I leave it to you."

I was surprised at God's answer:

"No, there are things I want to teach you; to set you free from your spiritual assumptions. I am not *contained* in any church, and it is not the only place to be baptized."

And so He continued to teach me; to widen my understanding of Himself and His ways; to set me free from man-made shackles. As a result I was baptized quietly and privately one day in a friend's bath, with two friends who also had been led to this point by God, without telling anyone. One was a Methodist and the other from the Salvation Army. It was simple obedience…a special occasion one Friday morning in April 1979, eighteen months after my conversion. Peace settled in my soul.

We moved as a family to the local Baptist church in 1983. I saw many baptisms and they all were thrilling events, powerful testimonies that often were instrumental in others coming into the Kingdom of God. At no point did I ever feel the need to be baptized again now that I had joined a Baptist church. And I was relieved that the pastor, when told, accepted my 'unconventional baptism' as perfectly valid.

February 1987 I was accepted into membership. Peter continued to keep a very low profile, and I had no idea where he stood with the Lord. He never shared a testimony of conversion with me. But whereas he had seemed, early on, to have been quietly neutral, even negative, now he seemed more passively accepting, but I couldn't figure out at all where he was spiritually. He had always been a man who kept his own counsel. I left that with God. It was His business, and Peter's.

Easter 1987 – In the midst of the Easter Day Praise Celebration which included a baptism service, God spoke quietly to me: "When Peter is baptized you will be baptized *publicly* with Him."

It was very clear and it was very simple. I had heard and I acknowledged to God that I had heard Him, but I did comment to the Lord that I couldn't *ever* see Peter doing something so public! But I did believe God had spoken to me. I kept these things in my heart, but on the surface I forgot about them. About five years later something triggered the memory and I shared with a couple of friends I knew that I could confide in, as a witness that I still believed God had spoken to me. I had no particular desire or feeling to be baptized publicly...if I had I don't think I would have waited for Peter to get around to it! And I let it all settle quietly back into my heart, wondering whether God could really bring that one to pass.

March 1995 and eight years had passed since hearing that word from God. Miguel Salamanca, our pastor friend from Mallorca, was in the UK for a week, ministering in the north of England. Before flying back he came to stay in Ashford for the weekend. What a blessing it was to have the opportunity to have some fellowship with this lovely man of God. Born in Mallorca, and brought up a Roman Catholic, he married an English girl, Cheryl. They became successful Night Club owners on the island, but the rest of their family life with their two children was somewhat stormy at times. Something had to give. God moved in and took hold of both of them, turned their lives around, delivered Miguel from alcoholism *instantly*, and they started a church in their home. That's where we met them, when on holiday in Mallorca in 1990. We had been many times on the receiving end of their generous hospitality, and it was good to give some back. We talked a lot and fellowshipped together; Miguel spent Sunday afternoon with some of the men in the church, and he shared in the evening service.

But it was after the service that the Holy Spirit started to move powerfully through this lovely pastoral man. Fred and

Madge, an elderly couple in the church, came up to talk to him and a crowd gathered to join in. Fred had recently come into church membership without being baptized, and we felt God had been speaking to us as a leadership for some months about restoring the biblical principle of commitment to Jesus Christ first by obedience in baptism, before commitment to the local church. We had kept praying for Fred to hear from God concerning baptism.

Out of the blue Miguel asked, in his Spanish accent –"Have you not been baptized as a believer, Fred?"

"No, I didn't think it was necessary. I was christened as a baby," Fred replied.

"So was I," said Miguel.

"I have been confirmed, too," says Fred.

"So have I," said Miguel. "Do you know what the Bible says, Fred?"

"Well…no," replied Fred.

"Come with me," said Miguel. And he picked up his Bible and took Fred to a back room. Five minutes later they returned, Fred beaming.

"I'm going to be baptized," he said.

Our mouths dropped open in astonishment. Madge, his wife, did a little dance, and gave voice to a "YIPPEE!" And Fred went off to tell the pastor his news.

Miguel turned to Peter – "Have you been baptized, Peter?" ('Miguel, this is a much harder nut to crack,' I thought.)

"I was baptized as a baby," Peter replied.

"Peter, have you not been baptized as a believer?"

"No, I don't think it is necessary."

"Sit down Peter; let me show you what it says in the Bible."

Miguel sat down beside him at the back of the church, and we gathered around and witnessed a man at work, flowing in the Spirit. He showed Peter two Scriptures – the one about Jesus' baptism, and Mark 16:16.

Concerning Jesus' baptism, Miguel said: "It wasn't necessary Pete, for Jesus to be baptized, but He did it to show *you* how!" ('Brilliant,' I thought!)

Then he said: "Now Peter, read Mark 16:16 out aloud."

Peter did that; Miguel asked him to read it again aloud, which he did:

> "*He who believes and is baptized will be saved, and he who does not believe will be condemned.*"

And then he stopped. I was sitting beside him, and as I looked at the side of my husband's face, I saw what looked like scales fall from his eyes…not physical scales of course, but what I saw was so powerful I saw it with *my* physical eyes. I held my breath. He repeated what he had read –

"'He who believes and is baptized…' – Heh! BELIEVING COMES BEFORE BAPTISM – I've never seen that before… The pastor has never taught this."

I interjected – "Yes he has, Pete, many times… it's just that you haven't seen it before. This is *your* moment; this is God's timing for *you*. He's just opened your eyes!"

Afterwards, bubbling with excitement, we wandered back to Thelma and Garry's where Miguel had been staying. Peter expressed his desire again to be baptized, and when pressed by Miguel for his testimony of conversion, he shared that back in 1982 he had asked Jesus to come into his life as Lord and Saviour. He was driving along on his motorbike to work at the time, and nearly came off it as a tremendous heat came upon him and surged through him.

Thelma, my prayer partner and friend, whispered in my ear – "What about you, Sue? Didn't God tell you all those years back to be baptized with Peter?"

I just looked at her and said nothing. Yes, I'd remembered – but I had been taken totally by surprise. Things had moved so quickly and I needed time to get my head round all of this. I felt in a state of shock… but I giggled as I considered that God indeed had a sense of humour!

Next, Miguel was on the phone to his wife, Cheryl, in Mallorca. She was over the moon about Peter getting baptized, and said – "And Sue with him!" We all had a quick chat with her and she repeated that to me too. I was shocked. I had not told either of them what God had spoken to me eight years before. But God was wasting no time to confirm His Word to me, and was basically saying: 'The time has come; don't prevaricate; it's time to move with this, Sue. *I am* speaking to you.'

The next day Peter and I sat in a café drinking coffee after our Sainsbury's shopping. And there, for the first time, I told him what God had spoken to me that Easter Sunday in 1987 – "When Peter is baptized, you will be baptized publicly with him." I was so surprised to see his eyes filling up with tears in such a public place…and I knew it was right. From that moment we were of one mind and most definitely in this together.

A few days later we went to see our pastor about being baptized together. That gave him a bit of a problem. Apparently it was just the day before that a woman who had been away from the Lord for a number of years but had now returned, wanted to make a fresh start by being baptized with her newly converted husband. Because he himself had publicly baptized her in the same church before, he refused her request but suggested that she publicly re-affirm her baptism vows at the next baptism service, when her husband was to be baptized. She agreed. And now a similar request in two days!

Although I had never been baptized as a believer publicly in church, or by him, he found himself in somewhat of a predicament, which I was certainly not slow to recognise. He had accepted my baptism in the bath by two friends as quite legitimate. I was now a deacon in the church leadership team, and no one can become a leader unless they have been baptized as a believer by total immersion. He didn't question that I had heard from God, but his predicament was on two levels – the couple he had just refused; and the possible confusion in the body of a church leader coming for baptism.

We both went off to pray about it and in the discussions that ensued we all agreed that *I simply wanted to obey God.* That was a matter of personal integrity; and the pastor made every effort to hold it all together and to find a way that would work for us all. He offered to stand me in the water with Peter – to baptize Peter, but not me.

We both were so grateful for that suggestion, not because we took it up…it was clear we mustn't, but because it clarified like nothing else could, the quality and simplicity of God's word to us. All this bending over backwards to find a compromise together was just that…a *compromise…a compromise on what God had simply said.* It felt right to take the pressure off the pastor, and it was right to put it right back in God's hands and ask Him to unfold His own plan for us. A burden was lifted and peace ruled in our hearts. We continued to pray and as things unfolded we kept the pastor informed along the way.

With clear heads and no personal agendas of how things *ought* to pan out, we were giving God room once again to speak. How patient He is with us all of the time. And how

quickly He responds. Peter and I checked one another out –
What is God saying to you? We both replied – "Mallorca!" We
checked it out with prayer partners and fellow leaders.
Unanimous! Not only a definite *yes* but also they'd all love to
be there!

We wrote to Miguel and Cheryl. They confirmed they
would be delighted to be involved. We set the date for Sunday
26th November 1995, during the morning service at La Vina
(English – The Vineyard – the church they pioneered and
pastored in Calla Mayor, Mallorca). Peter and I would be
baptized in the sea, and a fellowship celebration meal would
follow. It was decided that Roy and Miguel would baptize us.
Roy was over the moon – he felt it would be a great privilege,
and was as excited as the rest of us were!

September 1995 – I started feeling unwell. By the end of
the month, having nearly passed out on a couple of times in
church with the effort of singing hymns, I went and got my
blood pressure checked by the surgery nurse. It was within
normal limits. Hearing my symptoms, she got the duty doctor
to do an ECG. That produced a normal readout too. Initial
diagnosis was hormonal fluctuations…I'd already decided it
was my age!

I saw the doctor again in a month. I had the same problem
with no improvement. This time he muttered:

"You are too young for angina." He put me on HRT, told
me to go on a low-fat diet, and "come back in six weeks for a
cholesterol test." He also prescribed something to ease the
tension, tightness in my chest and the panic attacks. They call
the menopause the mid-life *crisis*…and so it is. Or so we
thought that's what it was, because – "You are too young for
angina," doc repeated again.

Our Mallorcan trip was a month away, and I felt in the middle of a real spiritual battle. In the spiritual realms *someone* didn't want me to go. As I became surer of this the more stubborn I became and the more certain I was going. So "On your bike!" was my response to an enemy who can't cope with *obedient* believers.

We travelled from Gatwick on 24th November with Garry and Thelma. It was so lovely to get away, and to be returning to what had become a favourite destination of ours. We stayed in the north of the island, at Puerto Pollenca. We began to relax immediately. Saturday was spent in lovely warm sunshine, walking in shorts and sunhats through the hills to the sea in the next valley. Sunday, the day of the baptism, was quite different – cooler, unsettled and a wee bit breezy. I had faxed Miguel and Cheryl several months before to say I'd had a picture of us being baptized in a rough sea, in a shower of rain. But whatever the weather the important thing was we were being baptized.

When we got to the Church, La Vina, the people were already praising God, so that when the service actually started there was a lovely spirit of praise moving and a sense of God's presence already there. All through the service the weather alternated between black clouds and showers, and sunny spells. As part of the baptism Peter and I had been asked to give a testimony in church, and then a public proclamation on the beach. Peter gave his testimony first, with Cheryl translating into Spanish for the Mallorceans. I had written my testimony down partly in English, partly in Spanish. I thought I'd make the effort, having been going to evening classes in Spanish. I assumed that the laughter and applause was appreciation of my effort, and not just hilarity over my mistakes! I won't include my testimony here because it appears elsewhere in the book.

But I finished with a simple prayer in Spanish, and I feel led by the Holy Spirit to include *that* here. It is so simple to speak, that there may be those reading this who also are studying Spanish in evening classes, who may like to use it themselves and be blessed in doing so, for I discovered that Spanish is a beautiful language of love and worship, and so easy to use in church when visiting Spain.

> *"Jesu es Senor. Te amo Jesu; te amo y bendigo tu nombre. Me rindo solo a ti Senor Jesu. Tu es mi Salvador, y mi Dios."* In English: "Jesus is Lord. I love you Jesus; I love you and bless your Name. I surrender alone to you Lord Jesus. You are my Saviour, and my God."

When the service of worship finished Peter and I, Miguel and Roy disappeared to change into white baptismal gowns. Now that was a sight! Then we led a procession of the congregation out of La Vina, across the main road of Calla Mayor, and down the road to the beach. Accompanied by guitars, we sang and praised God as we went. It was not cold by any means, but a very rough sea with sunshine and showers would describe conditions. I had seen this before. To the Mallorceans it was cold enough for coats and jumpers, but for us English it was shorts and T-shirts weather – temperatures in the mid-sixties at the end of November is very warm!

There were not many people around apart from some tourists on the beach, stopping to watch, and surfers in black wet suits having a break from the waves, and a number of people in the flats overlooking the beach watching from their windows and balconies. It felt good where we were, and what we were doing. We'd been asked to make a short public proclamation on the beach, and both of us did that using

Scriptures and a personal word. For some reason I thoroughly enjoyed that…maybe there's a hidden street evangelist inside me rearing to get out!

With that done we turned and walked into the sea, with the guitars leading songs of worship from the beach. The waves were huge, and I did wonder if we would get submerged *before* the moment. Miguel knew where to stop…he'd done this before, though never in a sea this rough apparently! For Roy it was his first baptism and I knew how very special this was for him. We turned to face the beach; Peter and I joined hands – we were going down *together*. Miguel carefully watched the swell and picked a huge wave, and led the baptism just as it passed us. There was such a back-drag of the wave that in seconds the wave was first at shoulder level, and then backing up at calf-level. As I went under, and the water level dropped, I knew my face hadn't got wet. I was momentarily disappointed – I wanted a proper burial! Should I speak up or keep quiet?

I decided to say – "My face didn't get wet." Roy agreed. So Miguel promptly took my left arm, and with Roy still on my right arm they dunked me again – and made sure I was totally immersed this time! What would the anti-rebaptism lobby feel about that – twice inside a minute! A strange thing happened. When my face went right under I *knew* my heart stopped beating. I recognised the feeling…it had happened before, and was one of the symptoms of a soon-to-be-diagnosed serious heart problem. There was no pain, but as I came out of the water I put my hand on my chest and stood motionless for a few moments, waiting. I missed about three beats and then it started thumping again, as if playing catch-up. It was back to normal after a couple of minutes.

Strangely enough, in the moment fear didn't come into it. I felt I had just *lived* the experience of Baptism to the full.

"Baptism is burial," St Paul says. Baptism symbolises dying to the old life, being buried, and rising up to the new life. My heart stopped... I 'died' for a moment, was buried under the water albeit for two seconds, and when I rose out of the water my heart started beating again. My memory still holds a powerfully graphic picture of the Truth, from that experience.

We all hugged one another in the middle of the battering waves, and then hand-in-hand we walked out of the sea to be greeted with great joy by all the others. I saw Ingrid talking to a couple of strangers. They turned out to be German tourists and she was able to share with them. They had been moved by what they had seen. As I moved amongst the people on the beach, I came across Garry chatting to two elderly ladies, and I joined them. They were fascinated by what they had witnessed and wanted to know more, and we had a real special time sharing with them. They were from the Faro Islands. Cheryl went up to a Spanish couple, who were standing on the fringe, and talked to them. They were traditionally Catholic, as most Spaniards are, but they did not have a living faith in Jesus Christ and they were challenged by the reality of our faith and the powerful symbolism of believer's baptism.

We eventually made our way back up the slipway and onto the main road to La Vina – dripping wet, but very happy. And the church had prepared a faith lunch for us. Lots of lovely fellowship followed, and eventually we got back to our hotel in time for the evening meal.

The weather was only stormy for that day...strange that! The next day was even warmer than before, and we drove down to our favourite beach and were in and out of the sea to keep cool!

Postscript. The following Sunday we were presented with our baptismal certificates in La Vina. But the big bonus was the Spanish couple Cheryl had talked with on the beach. They had been so challenged that they sought us out again, and turned up at church to find out more. Miguel was preaching, so he shared the full gospel, and called on the congregation for a response. Many of those already born again wanted the opportunity to recommit their lives to Jesus. So Miguel led in prayer, and they did just that. And what of the new Spanish couple? They prayed too, and for the first time committed their lives to Jesus Christ.

That, for Peter and I, was 'the icing on the cake,' to use an English expression. God sealed our obedience to *public* baptism…more public than we had imagined, by blessing other people's lives as a result of our obedience. Our gratitude to Him still overflows at the remembrance of it.

Chapter 9

MIXED REACTIONS

Thanks be to God, Who always leads us in triumphal procession in Christ and through us spreads everywhere the fragrance of the knowledge of Him. For we are to God the aroma of Christ among those who are being saved and those who are perishing. To the one we are the smell of death, to the other, the fragrance of Life. 2 Corinthians 2: 14-16

WAS I BEING A WEE BIT NAÏVE to expect everyone to enthuse at the news of my new life in Christ? Yes – and no. Yes, because I was a thirty-year-old woman – a wife, mother and a secondary school teacher. I had gained enough experience of life to realise that learning to cope with the ups and downs in life, taking the rough with the smooth, was a big part of the process of maturing from youth to adulthood. Some never manage it, and the sight of say a balding middle-aged man having a tantrum because he can't have his own way, is not a pretty sight.

But also *no*, I wasn't being naive. Jesus said that no one could enter the Kingdom of God unless he became as a little child. I had been born again; I was beginning a new life from the beginning. Spiritually I was a little child, and a little child is always so trusting. That, I believe, is what Jesus meant. I had come to the Cross, trusted God as my Father, and Jesus as

59

my Saviour and Lord. I simply trusted God with my life from that moment. That is childlikeness, not naivety. I was so happy at the treasure I had found that I wanted to tell others, especially those important to me. I wanted to share what I had, with them… for God's Love can't be measured and will never run out!

So was I surprised by those first reactions to my 'good news'? Yes, I was – good or bad – they *all* surprised me! First, there was the Rev. Christopher Woods, priest-in-charge of the church I was attending. When I tried to put into words what had just happened to me, he simply said: "Oh, that was the Holy Spirit welling up within you, and overflowing out of your mouth."

Wow, that encouraged me!

Then there was Peter, my husband, about an hour later. He looked a little scared, and offered to make me a cup of tea with lots of sugar! His hand was shaking as he gave it to me. I think he was in a state of shock! He made no comment, but listened to my short testimony. Chalk and cheese are Peter and I. He's the introvert, I'm the extrovert. I talk, he listens.

I saw a gradual change in him over the next few years. He started coming to church regularly; he agreed to have the occasional home group in our home, and that became a regular event. Sometimes I would catch him watching me with a smile on his face when I was sharing or sometimes leading. I guess he looked proud, but he kept his own counsel. When I asked him about it or whether he would like to speak and share in the group, he said: "I prefer to listen to *you*…you have a real gift there with the Bible."

That was encouragement indeed. He kept his own counsel about his own faith, and never let on where he stood with God. I was mighty curious but knew him well enough not to push.

Then out of the blue one day in Mallorca we were sitting having tea with a lady from La Vina (Miguel and Cheryl's church), and she asked him: "Peter, when were you converted to Jesus?"   And I heard his testimony for the first time! Apparently four or five years after my conversion he was riding his motorbike to work one day, when he simply asked Jesus to come into his life and take control. He suddenly felt as though he had been set on fire...he was so overwhelmed by the heat inside him that he very nearly came off his motorbike! My heart leapt for joy. Still waters indeed run deep with the introvert who keeps his own counsel. His testimony was well worth waiting for!

The morning after my conversion and baptism with the Spirit I awoke suddenly just before dawn, and somebody definitely spoke to me. I lay still for a minute or so and felt icy cold. Death was in the air. I'd felt the same coldness the night my dad died. A voice spoke: "What have you done? What have you done? Stop it now before you go too far and you won't be able to get back." I'd not heard this voice before, but I realised it wouldn't be the last time that the devil would speak to me, so I might as well get things straight at the outset. I replied: "Be quiet. I won't listen to you. I belong to Jesus now. *Be quiet in Jesus' Name.*" I took my Bible and opened it somewhere...anywhere, and kept reading by the growing dawn light, until the cold went away, and the new resident inside me warmed me up until I glowed all over, felt a great Peace, and was overwhelmed by the Love of God.

Next day brought another reaction. I was having tea with my friend Christine, who lived just around the corner on the same estate. She had become a friend as a result of her husband, Gerry, working with Peter in the same bank, and also because we got pregnant at the same time. Our two oldest children were at school, but we continued to meet as we had done to let the three remaining pre-schoolers play together whilst we had a natter. I arrived after lunch as arranged. The children immediately got together and I joined Chris in the kitchen whilst she prepared the drinks. A couple of times she looked at me intently. Drinks made, we sat down together in the lounge and started to chat. She looked at me strangely again, and this time I thought – 'surely it's not that obvious!'

She spoke: "Sue, there is something different about you – what has happened? I've not seen you like this before, and I feel somewhat envious, and I don't know why. Come on, tell me!"

First I pressed her to explain what it was she thought was different. She said that my face was glowing, I seemed so happy, and there was something 'powerful' about me.

I was overwhelmed at such a confirmation of what had happened, and with great joy I simply shared my testimony. She kept asking me questions…she was so hungry to know more. And I was more than willing to keep answering. This is what the Bible calls 'witnessing', I thought, and the Scripture that was preached the night before was being fulfilled right here and now. *Jesus said: "But when the Holy Spirit comes upon you, you will receive power and you will be my witnesses…"* *(Acts 1:8).* POWER TO WITNESS – that is what I received last night when I was baptised in the Holy Spirit. What a relief; what a joy! There is no self-effort required to witness – it just flows naturally, or should I say supernaturally naturally!

Chris wanted what I had.

"Just ask Jesus," I said. "Talk to Him; He'll show you. What I've just shared with you is unique to me. What He's got for you is unique to you. Talk to Him, Chris…he does answer prayer."

And He did. Chris and Gerry had short notice of a move, and they were gone from Ashford in just a few weeks. It was a job move with the bank to Southampton. Later they moved again, this time to Gloucester. From the occasional contact I had with Chris I knew she was seeking…and in my heart I knew she would find. A Scripture that had become familiar to me was – *"Ask and it will given to you, seek and you will find, knock and the door will be opened to you." (Luke 11:9)* I knew it was a matter of time, and His timing is perfect!

It was at least six years after that memorable sunny afternoon spent with Chris. Peter and I had just become a permanent venue for a church House Group. Marion, one of the deacons, was leading the group. We were coming to the end of the Bible study part when the phone rang. In those days we only had a corded phone and it was in the room we were in, so there was no going away for privacy in order that the group could carry on. I was intending to say to the caller that we had a meeting in progress and I would call them back. I didn't know who it was…no Caller Display in those days!

"It's Chris."

"Chris?" I asked. I didn't recognise the voice…she sounded very excited.

"Yes, it's Chris Train, Sue, and I've got some news for you. You are the first person that came to mind, and I had to ring and tell you."

My spirit leapt inside of me. It was one step ahead of my brain.

"Yes Chris, lovely to hear from you. What is it?"

She proceeded to tell me that she had persuaded her friend to go with her to the Billy Graham Crusade in Bristol, and they had both gone forward and committed their lives to Jesus

Christ. With the excited voice coming through the receiver, and all my exclamations of 'great', 'wonderful', 'hallelujah', and earnest questions for more details, I realised the House Group had gone *very* quiet, and were listening intently. I heard Marion's voice say: "Someone's been converted!" followed by more whoops of joy and 'hallelujahs' from the group. Chris could hear this so I told her what was going on and we would indeed be praying for her and her friend in a moment.

She finished the conversation: "I'll let you go, Sue. I knew you were the right person to ring. I knew you would understand and rejoice with me. Thank you, Sue. I'll write to you."

Another move followed. Gerry was moved by the bank to work in Bath. And it was here that Chris' husband, Gerry, made *his* commitment to Jesus, and Peter and I had the joy of going to Bath and seeing then getting baptised as believers... full immersion in Manvers Street Baptist Church. Baptism is indeed 'burial', as the Scripture says.

Chapter 10

MORE REACTIONS

*Coming to His hometown He began
teaching...And they took offence at Him. But
Jesus said to them: "Only in his home town and
in his own house is a prophet without honour."
And He did not do many miracles there because
of their lack of faith. Matthew 13:54-58*

AND SO IN LESS THAN TWENTY-FOUR HOURS I
had reactions from my priest, my husband, the devil, and
a friend, and looked back in retrospect and seen fruit produced
by God out of the testimony of a day-old babe in Christ! What
an amazing, wonderful God we have. And overwhelmed by
His Love for me, my heart was on fire with love for him. I'd
never been on the receiving end of such Love, and I'd never felt
a love like this pouring out of my heart. I had simply fallen in
love with Jesus...my Saviour, my Lord, my God.

Reactions to this change in my life continued, and continue
to this day and will do so until I go to be with Him. And then
all things will be perfect. But until then Jesus taught much in
His Word to prepare His disciples for the reactions they will
come up against. He encouraged them, warned them, and
equipped them to deal with the two extremes – hero worship,
and rejection – both tools in the hand of the enemy designed to

steal, kill or destroy not only their faith but even their lives –
and every reaction in between.

The next reaction was just as lively as that of my friend
Chris, but not for the same reasons. The following day we
drove over the border into Sussex to have lunch with my sister
and family. These were regular reciprocal visits between the
families, enjoyed by all, particularly with the five lively
children present!

It was important to me that I told my sister my news. I had
been brought up in a family that liked a lively discussion,
debated almost everything, and were pretty open and honest
with each other. But I waited until I was alone with her, and
simply shared my testimony with her of my conversion and
baptism in the Holy Spirit. I can remember specifically saying:
"I have received the most precious gift of all...the gift of the
Holy Spirit." I assumed she would understand, she being nine
years older than me, totally committed to her Anglican faith,
and I remember mother telling me that my sister once
considered becoming a nun.

She looked shocked, and asked me what I meant, and
suggested we go for a walk together to chat. We left
immediately, leaving the men tackling the washing up. I
answered her questions by briefly telling her what had
happened recently. I didn't really have any chance to go much
into the history of it all, because she'd by now built up quite a
head of steam and it blew. She said that I had betrayed the
church; she meant the Anglo Catholic church that we both had
been brought up in, in South Wales, and where we had both
been christened and confirmed. What had I done? Who had
led me astray? Had I joined some strange group...a cult or
something? I sensed fear, anger and rejection all tangling up

inside of her. I kept my cool, but was amazed and not a little baffled at such an extreme reaction.

No, I hadn't joined any strange group. In fact, God had been doing business with me for the past eighteen months and I had not whispered a thing to a living soul. What He had started to do in my life had been so precious and beautiful that I hadn't wanted it to be trampled on by anyone wearing big boots! I had now simply given my life to Jesus Christ, taken Him as my Saviour and Lord, and with the Holy Spirit inside me my religion had been transformed into a wonderful relationship.

I hadn't been looking for it, or for God. I'd thought I was a 'grown-up' Christian already, because of my religion, but God found me and showed me what was on His heart. What an awesome God and wonderful Father He is!

There was no calming my sister though – she was upset and angry. She was clearly anxious too that if I didn't reconsider, then the spiritual gulf that had just opened up between us, by what I had shared, might draw our paths further apart. It was already clear that we were going in different directions spiritually. Would it affect our sibling relationship too? I prayed not and I am sure she felt the same.

This was the first test of my new found faith, and although I felt a profound sense of grief at my sister's reaction, I found my faith strengthened for having gone through this particular testing. We are told as Christians to expect all sorts of trials; in fact, the practice of 'easy believism' that says – Come to Jesus and all your troubles will be over – is a lie, a travesty of the Truth. You actually pick up a host of different problems! A Scripture that became a favourite Word of encouragement for me in the early years was *1 Peter 1:3-9 '.... though now for a little while you may have had to suffer grief in all kinds of trials. These have come so that your faith – of greater worth*

than gold which perishes even though refined by fire – may be
proved genuine and may result in praise, glory and honour
when Jesus Christ is revealed.' (Vs. 6/7)

Next was a weekend trip to friends Jean and Paul and children who lived near the coast of Essex not far from Clacton. Jean and I were friends from schooldays. So we now continue a friendship that has survived more than fifty-five years. This visit was about two weeks after my conversion and eighteen months after my dad's death, and I had spoken to no one, not even this old friend. She too had been brought up Anglo Catholic and went to the same church as my sister and I. After my experience with my sister, I wondered how she would react to my news and prayed it wouldn't be as tough.

On our arrival we poured over the Chinese takeaway menu and made our selection. Once we had filled our plates and started to eat I ventured out tentatively with: "I've got something to tell you."

Jean looked at me intently, and before I spoke further she said: "I know, and I think I know what it's about."

"Yes?" I said, very curious and a sense of expectation rising within me.

"It has something to do with God, and your dad's death, hasn't it? When I saw you after your dad died you had such a peace about you...I had never seen you like that before. And I was envious, and I wanted whatever it was you had."

An animated discussion followed which did all of us the world of good! But this time the encouragement was mutual – I was so encouraged that Jean had recognised accurately that some big change had occurred in my life when my dad died; and she was really encouraged to discover, this particular evening, that she had been spot-on with her discernment. My faith and confidence went up a few notches, and Jean's hunger for spiritual reality had grown.

They moved to Nottingham not long afterwards to take up new jobs in the medical profession. They joined a church in the city. I had prayed that God's hand would be on them, and it surely was! Jean was so excited. This was just what she needed at this stage in her search for reality with God. This was an Anglican church that had been renewed in the Holy Spirit. It was vibrant with the Life of God. So many churched and unchurched people were coming in, hearing the Gospel of Salvation, and receiving Jesus Christ as their personal Lord and Saviour, that they were baptizing more believers than they were christening babies. There were prayer groups, study groups, healing services, worship groups, and 'Know Jesus' groups. That last one rang bells with me. Hadn't Colin Urquhart, in the late seventies, started Know Jesus groups in the church he was vicar of after he himself had an encounter with God, was baptized in the Holy Spirit and spoke in tongues?

Yes he had, and he had visited this Nottingham church on several occasions, and had been God's instrument in bringing renewal in the Spirit here, and it had adopted the Know Jesus groups, having heard of the tremendous success they had been in Colin's church and many other churches.

So Jean joined a Know Jesus group. During a communion service in one of the meetings God's timing was perfect yet again, and she had an encounter with the Saviour, and was filled to overflowing with the Holy Spirit. Out of her mouth came the overflow – surprised by God, she was speaking in tongues! Such Joy…such Peace!

One more reaction…or two, sort of! A few days later Peter and I went, as we usually did, to the Harvest Supper at Alkham.

He'd lived there with his mother, Vera, before we met and married and moved to Ashford.

I loved Vera dearly. She was a lovely lady…kind and generous, always busy helping people. I thanked God for such a great mum-in-law. She lived alone on a farm in the Alkham Valley, having run it with her husband, Charlie, for many years. She had been widowed for about seventeen years and arthritis was taking its toll, but she kept going and kept busy and was very much liked by many people.

I sat between Peter and his mum for the Harvest Supper in the village hall. I hadn't had a chance as yet to say anything to her, so I launched out with the question – "Mum, who do you love most of all."

I thought this was the best way to open the conversation because I was so in the first flush of zeal as a new Christian that if someone had popped that question to me I would have jumped back enthusiastically with – "Jesus!"

When she answered, "Well, I love you all the same dear," she was simply being 'Granny', and being absolutely fair to all her children and grandchildren! A very wise answer, but not the one I was looking for!

She looked at me enquiringly, so I thought I'd better finish what I started. I briefly told her that I had come to know Jesus and loved Him more than anyone or anything else. She smiled and with the grace that old people sometime display, she simply said: "How lovely for you my dear, that's very special."

The next day we were in Alkham Church to see the flower festival, and what a breathtakingly beautiful feast for the eyes and nose that was…many labours of love.

As I was walking around slowly, enjoying it all immensely, the vicar's wife came up to me. She smiled at me and said quietly: "You've got converted to Jesus Christ, haven't you?"

Momentarily taken by surprise, my mouth dropped open, but I was not slow to answer: "Yes, I have, but how did you know?"

"I was talking to your mother-in-law this morning and she said that you had gone all religious!"

I insisted that was the last thing that had happened…quite the opposite.

She replied: "Oh, I know that, Sue, I knew what had happened to you as soon as she told me. Praise the Lord!"

"Praise the Lord indeed! You obviously knew from your own personal experience?"

"Yes I do. Be encouraged Sue – I'll be praying for you."

None of these encounters with different people were accidental or a mistake. I saw them then, and even more so now as 'God encounters.' In other words, He knew all about them before they happened, and I grew spiritually as a result of those early encounters. That was His intention.

I look back and see something so important, a big lesson…a matter of life and death. Concerning Jesus Christ there is 'Religion' and 'Relationship'. A man may practice his religion all his life, but if he never enters into a Relationship with Jesus Christ then he is as lost and without hope, just as much as a man in the street who wants nothing to do with God. Jesus Himself said: *"And this is Eternal Life Father, that they may KNOW You, the only True God, and Jesus Christ Whom You have sent." (John 17:3).* The key word is *'know'*.

Creedal belief is not enough for salvation. Personal knowledge is essential. The word for 'know', used here by Jesus, is an intimate *knowing*, as a man knows his wife. And that speaks of an intimate and passionate love relationship with Jesus Christ. For thirty years I had religion. Then an encounter with the Living God was the beginning of a beautiful love relationship with Him...Father, Son, and Holy Spirit, and it was always His initiative. I began to see, from my own experience, a clash between religion and relationship. It doesn't have to be that way. The two can work in perfect harmony. *BUT* this is only possible in the Spirit, when the religion we practice is a religion of the Spirit. Without the Holy Spirit in charge, the religion we practice will be ruled by a religious spirit, which is *not* holy in any sense. It will be harsh and legalistic, critical of other churches and believers, and produces death, not Life. From those early days God has given me His burden for the lost, not only those outside the church but in the church also.

I make no apologies for saying that if you look around the church of Jesus Christ and are honest about the poor state it is in you can see that religion can and does hijack real faith, real prayer, real repentance, real Love, real salvation...and much more.

I leave you with a question: Which church do you belong to?

If your answer is – the Methodist church or the Catholic Church or the Anglican Church, or the Pentecostal church or... Then ponder on your answer and mine and consider what God desires here.

"Which church do you belong to, Sue?"

"There's more than one?"

Chapter 11

THE CHILDREN

*O Lord, our Lord, how majestic is Your Name in
all the earth! You have set Your Glory above the
heavens. From the lips of children and infants
You have ordained praise. Ps.8: 1/2*

THE BIRTH OF A CHILD has to stand out as *the* event
of a lifetime. To be there, either doing all the hard work,
or observing the event and assisting in whatever way is needed,
it never diminishes as mysterious, and miraculous, and
wonderful. And whether you have a religion or none, you
cannot help but sense that something or someone greater than
yourselves has a hand in it. Husband and wife come to the
decision to: "Let's make babies!" But God has already been at
work providing the equipment to make it all possible! If we do
our part, then God does His. He is in the business of producing
life…He is the Giver of Life. That is what I sensed the moment
I knew I was pregnant for the first time. A miracle had
happened in my body before I realised it. The first sign to me
was feeling sick every day!

Then the birth seals the reality of it all. After nine months
carrying this precious growing life inside…the moment arrives.
All thoughts of morning sickness, indigestion, odd pains, funny
food fads, and the pushing and panting and sweating preceding
the birth…all these are forgotten when this tiny bundle of

precious life fills his lungs with a loud cry and is placed into your arms. It's not been easy and in retrospect you know it's not all going to be a smooth road ahead as this bundle of joy grows up through your sleepless nights, his 'tantrum two's', scrapes and breaks, teenage angst, finding out the dangers for himself – not listening to your sound advice, making mistakes big and small, breaking hearts and having his own heart broken, breaking yours also along the way. But nothing…but nothing, can take away the joy of the miracle of his birth all those years ago!

I have mentioned our two children but once so far, and that was in chapter two, to note their names and their dates of birth. Ian Frederick and Christine Anne came in that order three years and three months apart. In September 1977 when I was converted to Jesus Christ and filled with the Holy Spirit, they were in their sixth and third years respectively. I cannot remember actually sitting them down and telling them the big change that had happened in my life, but the way I lived my daily life changed even in the smaller details. And praying and reading the Bible became the norm, as well as regularly going to church and attending the mid-week Bible Study at the 'vicarage'. Ian was a typical 'man' and kept things mostly to himself (just like his dad really!), but I sensed he had quietly taken on board for himself something of what had happened to his mum and he was enthusiastic in his involvement with things for the younger people in church life.

Christine was different. She was that much younger, a pre-schooler who was at home all day with mum, except for a couple of mornings a week at playschool, and therefore was even more aware and influenced by what she saw of her mum's new life with Jesus. She asked lots of questions about God and Jesus and prayer…she started praying little prayers at bedtime, and sometimes when I was tucking her in she would ask me to stay and pray with her.

Then one night, when she was just over four years old, and I was kissing her goodnight with the words 'Goodnight and God bless you', as I always did, she demanded my full attention. She obviously had something important to tell me.

"What is it?" I asked.

"I've decided I want to walk with Jesus and go to Heaven with Him," she replied.

"That's wonderful, Chris, He'll love that. Do you want to do that now?"

"Yes, now," she said.

"So you want to walk with Jesus all your life, do you, and go all the way to Heaven with Him?"

"Yes."

"Well, you talk to Jesus and tell Him what you have just told me. And I will do a little thank you prayer when you have finished."

And she closed her eyes, was quiet for a bit and then she reached her hand up into the air and asked Jesus if He would hold her hand so that she could walk with Him, and be with Him always, and walk to Heaven with Him. There was a sizeable lump in my throat when I said 'amen' with her, and thanked the Lord Jesus that He had answered her prayer.

She started school a few months later. Ian was nearly eight and in Junior school, beginning to feel his feet, wanting to be acceptable with his peer group, beginning to speak with an Ashford accent, and trying out on us new words he had picked up to see if we reacted! We did! He did not know what they meant, but we did!

Christine enjoyed school, told her headmistress that she was a Christian, and was delighted at the very kind response she got back, when the Head asked Chris if she loved Jesus. When Chris said "Yes", the head replied, "I do too!" What a lovely response to such a tender-aged child. Her new faith could so easily have been damaged by a less sensitive reply. But she came as a child and trusted this adult in authority. She could come no other way. She was only five years old. And that is why Jesus speaks to us, I believe, about coming to Him as a child…just in simple trust of Him. He knows that we adults complicate things…so He exhorts us – "Come as a child." It is so important…and it defines our future in eternity.

A few years passed during which Chris was enjoying Sunday school, and Ian moved from Sunday school to a Youth group. Ian continued to keep his thoughts on spiritual things to himself, whilst Christine was full of questions about the Bible and God. Two totally different personalities, but God had His hand on them both.

Then over a period of about six months all sorts of exciting things happened. First there was Ian at just about thirteen years. One Sunday morning after the service, in which a missionary spoke about their work in India, Ian declared that God had spoken to him during the talk and told him that one day He was going to send him to India to build bridges. Wow, thrilling stuff! I pondered – 'Concrete bridges, Lord, or spiritual bridges?'

No reply! It was not for me to know, but for God to reveal the time and the details to Ian in His good and perfect time.

A month or so later, the youth group were taken to a Youth Weekend being held in a church in Hastings, just down the coast from us here in Ashford, and Ian was looking forward to going. Sunday evening came and we were watching TV. I heard a car pull up and a door slam. Our gate creaked and the back door opened and we looked up to see Ian standing still in the dining room, looking at us. It was only a few seconds before he spoke, but what I saw made my heart skip a beat. He looked radiant…his eyes looked as though lights had been switched on in them. And really that is just what had happened. He took a big breath and launched into what he must say:

"Mum and dad, I thought that I was already a Christian. But it was all on the outside; but now I am a *real* Christian; I have my own faith now and it's on the inside, and it's the real thing."

We were amazed and overjoyed. We wanted to know all the details but Ian was obviously overwhelmed by what had happened to him, and he went quietly off to bed. I understood what he meant, and realised he now needed to be afforded plenty of room to work out his own faith with God.

A surprising reaction to this came from Christine. She was certainly quiet the next day, but when three days had passed and she definitely wasn't her usual chatty self I knew there was something not quite right that may need some delicate handling. So on the third day after Ian's momentous news I managed to get alone with her in her bedroom and gently asked her if there was anything she was worried about. She seemed relieved to be asked – it was not her nature to bottle things up. When she had heard about Ian's experience of God at the Youth Weekend, she began to have doubts that she was a Christian at all. Why, I asked? Because she had never had any experience of God like that. She was in a crisis and I'm glad we hadn't left it any longer. She needed a serious dose of encouragement and reassurance, which I was able to give her, and her old cheerful and full-of-fun nature returned. And I learned some important lessons about God's dealings with people. Just as no two snowflakes are the same, each person is different too, and God deals with each of us differently and uniquely, and very *personally*. And our first dealings with Him is just that...the first. There are many more to come. I went through a stage when someone thought I could have done better and I owned the phrase – *God hasn't finished with me yet!*

How God loves a childlike heart. If only we would watch children relating to God and learn lessons from them. Ian stuck his neck out when he shared that God had spoken to him about India, and then God met with him and blessed him abundantly at the Youth weekend. Christine was honest about her heartache concerning how her brother's experience had challenged her own faith...if there was more, she wanted more!

How pivotal that was in her life, because soon afterwards something happened that was going to steer the direction of her future. It was a Sunday morning that was to be a celebration of believers' baptism. Chris had a front row seat with her friends from the primary Sunday school group. During prayer led by the Pastor at the end of the service I looked up and saw Chris had a bright red face, and she seemed to be fidgeting somewhat. As I looked I sensed that God was speaking to her. I wondered if it was about being baptised – the Holy Spirit turns up big time at such occasions, and it is a very powerful time of praise and worship, and testimony to the Glory of God. Perhaps that was it. But, I thought...she's a bit young, isn't she Lord? No answer.

And so, a couple of hours later we found ourselves sitting around the table enjoying Sunday lunch.

"Chris, did God speak to you this morning in church?"

"Yes He did."

"Was it about being baptised?"

"No, but I went straight to the Pastor in the vestibule afterwards and told him what God had said. I thought that was the right thing to do."

"Yes it was. So what did you tell him?"

"I told him that God had spoken to me and told me that one day He would send me to be a missionary in Russia."

"That's amazing, Chris! But do you know that they do not allow Christian missionaries into Russia?"

"Well, they will when I'm meant to go."

Her answer stopped me in my tracks, and my own growing faith was yet again soundly challenged by the faith of a child.

Another big lesson she taught me along the road, toward the inevitable trip to Russia, was that God would do His part, which is impossible for man, but we must get on with our part in preparation for His call…practical action is very much a part of our preparation for a call which God puts on our life for some future date. And Chris did exactly this. First she started to learn the basics of Russian. We owned an early computer – an Amstrad CPC 6128. She created a Russian alphabet, using what was called an Art Master programme, and she used some old notes of mine, from my last year at school when I filled in some spare time with some Russian lessons.

Then when she got into the Lower Sixth form at Grammar school she said she would like to learn Russian, and one of the language teachers who knew some Russian was willing to run a GCSE General Russian Studies course which Chris thoroughly enjoyed and passed.

And so she left Highworth School and took up a place at Keele University near Stoke on Trent, where she started a joint degree course in Music and Russian. She was still on track with God, though He had not spoken further on the matter as yet.

As part of her Russian degree she spent a whole year out, studying at the Technical University in St Petersburg. She felt an immediate love for 'Mother Russia' – a confirmation of her call twelve years before. God brought some Russian Christians across her path and she was able to enjoy friendship and the fellowship she desperately needed. She was invited to a conference in St Petersburg where she met with some 'Omers', people serving with OM[1] in Russia. God was beginning to put His Plan into place, even if she couldn't see it clearly yet.

Well, where are the children now?

The summer of 1997 was a big crossroads in both their lives, but for very different reasons. Ian was sectioned under the Mental Health Act and admitted to a psychiatric unit in St Albans in the August. A few weeks later Christine went off to Holland for a preparation and orientation conference before joining OM on one of its mission ships – the *Doulos* – and sailing off into the sunset to serve the Lord in Far Eastern realms.

Ian had strayed off the path the Lord had set him on at the age of thirteen; he had taken a wrong turn at a crossroads in his life less than a year after his conversion; and by the age of eighteen, when he went off to Hatfield Polytechnic to study Civil Engineering, he was rushing headlong into trouble…dabbling in those things to which parents say "Don't do it" – things in the world common to teenagers down the

---

[1] Operation Mobilisation – an Evangelical Christian outreach organisation founded in 1957 to mobilise young people to live and share the Gospel of Jesus, an organisation that transforms lives and communities over 110 countries, bringing a message of hope to the people of the worlds, largely by means of two ocean-going ships. Website: www.uk.om.org

generations. Some get through this rite of passage unscathed and all the wiser, some do not. Ian didn't. Drugs were his downfall. He was sectioned four times between 1997 and 2005. The last time was triggered by his fiancée calling off their marriage two months before the event. It had been five years since he had last been sectioned. He loved being in a family of his own; he's not a loner; he was in love, and he cherished the building of a relationship with his fiancée's little boy. Then suddenly it was all over.

He is rebuilding his life now; he's older and wiser in his late thirties. He's still on medication and will be for the foreseeable future, and only God knows what that may hold. But as I continue praying for my son, God has given me such reassurance that through all these years He has never let Ian go. Only He knows the end from the beginning. He is *the* God of miracles, and I trust Him. Ian recently spoke to me with a smile – "Thanks for putting in a word for me, Mum." My reply – "It's a privilege, Ian!"

Both the children are constantly in our prayers. And I know that God answers prayer, sometimes in ways that surprise us, but His timing is perfect. He is a wonderful Father and so patient with us and He waits to welcome home His prodigal son. I place my son in his hands and I trust Him implicitly. He still has a word to fulfil in Ian's life and I wonder if maybe one day he *will* be building bridges in India!

Christine had finished her degree course at Keele with a 2-1 Honours degree. She already knew that her encounter with OM in Russia was no coincidence. God's leading was for her to sail with the *MV Doulos*. I prayed to the Lord: "What about your call to send her to Russia?" He gave me a clear understanding He would send her to Russia later on; that her term of service on the ship would serve to prepare her, strengthen her faith, toughen her up and equip her for what would be a difficult place to live and work, and without Him – an impossible place.

She served over three years on the *Doulos* and the things God taught are her *own* testimony. But what a privilege we felt to witness the maturing of our daughter as a Christian as she saw half the world, working with perhaps thirty different nationalities on the ship, making enduring and precious friendships, serving God in so many cultures that she gained unique insight into the hearts and minds of so many people in the world, and not least, of course, the privilege she had of seeing so many people around the world hungry for God and coming to a saving knowledge of Jesus Christ. The example of three hundred 'Doulois' living in love and harmony together, and the Word they brought about God so loving the world that He gave His only Son…was so powerful, that God did and continues to use it to draw peoples of the world to Himself.

When God was ready to send Chris to Russia He told her, and confirmed it, and she was sure. She spent nearly four years in Russia, with God giving her His love for the place and the people. Then He began to loosen her roots and she knew she would be on the move again before long. God's timing, with personal and family situations, brought her back to the UK on compassionate leave, as her brother was sectioned for the third time a few months after his marriage plans were cancelled.

Her planned two weeks turned into several months as it became apparent that she herself was suffering from 'burnout'…a price many missionaries pay. She went up to Carlisle for a break. This is where the OM International office is sited. She was befriended and loved and cherished and counselled by OMers there who understood, and who were able to give her space to recover and a prescription of a little admin in the office as therapy, without the stress of responsibility. It worked. Through the loving attention she got, God slowly brought her out of the depression that accompanied the burnout and did a beautiful work of healing in her life. Looking back I think it is true that when God is doing the mending we become strong in those broken places that He has healed. Praise His Name!

Not another coincidence… no – God's perfect timing yet again. Whilst in Carlisle Chris learned that the PA to the International Director of Operation Mobilisation, Peter Maiden, was considering leaving at the end of the year. Christine's heart leapt at that news. She'd love that sort of work. She made it known to Peter that if the position became vacant she would like to be considered for it. Could God be speaking to her? Yes, of course He could… and He was. He had planned it. Some time later Peter asked Chris if she would consider prayerfully if it was right for her to take over the position of his PA. She didn't rush in, but soon came back with a 'yes' answer. And nearly six years later she is still Peter's PA. She loves the work; she's one of those unusual people who love administration. I said to her once it was listed in the Scriptures as a spiritual gift from God. And she reckoned that was what she must have!

So – the children? Both of them were called by God in their tender years. Both of them have taken quite different paths so far. Both of them still have some surprises to come from God. He loves them both; Jesus died for them both; He doesn't look on one as a success and the other as a failure…that's the world's way of looking at us – *not* God's. Both are unfinished vessels in God's hands. He hasn't let either of them go. And with Him the best is always still to come. Glory!

But there are actually more than two children under our parental jurisdiction. There are actually six altogether. Apart from our own two, Peter and I between us are godparents to four children. They are all grown up now…some single, others married, some with children of their own.

Personally for those who would feel I have had but a small spiritual input into their lives, I can only say that geographical distances may be a reason but not an excuse. But I assure them all that I have been often in prayer for them – with them in spirit, even though at a distance physically. I pray that this book may find its way into each of their hands and provide insight into my desires for them, and gratitude for having known them and been blessed by them all in many different ways.

And so to Ian, Christine, Megan, David, Thomas, and Abigail, my enduring prayer for you is that, if you don't yet know Jesus, you will come to know Him who loved you and died for you on the Cross – to know Jesus your God as your own personal Saviour and Lord. And for those of you who met Him and knew Him once, but your heart has grown cold toward Him and you have lost your way, that you would call on His Name, and He *will* answer you and bring you home.

And for those of you who have walked with Him, serving Him constantly over the years but have grown weary and lost the fervour and enthusiasm that you had at first, may you hear His lovely voice calling you to return to that first love for the Bridegroom Who once set you on fire for Him with His passionate Love for you. I speak to you from my heart because I've been along all these paths myself and proved Him to be a Faithful God and Lover of my soul.

I draw this chapter to a close with a testimony concerning one of these children that is sweet and simple and beautiful, and I cannot resist including it. Even without naming any names it remains to me one of those treasured lessons from God, through an innocent child, to a 'grown-up'.

At six years old this child already had begun to develop a love for music and singing. One evening she was in the bath and I was in a nearby room making up a bed. She was singing and humming as she played with the plastic boats and ducks, and I wasn't actually listening. It was my spirit that reacted first...a flood of joy rippled through me and got my attention! Then I heard it...this little child was singing in the Spirit. It was a beautiful song and I stopped and listened and it blessed me to bits. I didn't recognise the song – it seemed to have a life of its own. Ripples of joy continued as I listened. I tiptoed out of the bedroom and towards the bathroom. I could see her playing with the boats but she didn't see me coming. Totally absorbed in her singing, it wasn't until I was standing next to the bath silently enjoying one of those surprise moments from God, that she realised I was there. She looked up, stopped singing, and smiled at me coyly.

I asked: "Did you know what you were singing?"

"No," was the reply.

"Do you like singing like that?"

"Yes I do. It makes me feel good."

"Do you sing like that anywhere else?"

"Yes I do, in church and in school. I sometimes can't read the words in the hymn book quickly enough, so I sing with my own words."

"Do you know where the words come from?" I asked.

"God gives them to me," was the child's reply.

> *Jesus said: "I tell you the Truth, unless you change and become like little children, you will never enter the Kingdom of Heaven." Matthew 18:3*

How many times I have tried to be *so* adult even when I knew this Truth, and I've worn myself out! My Heavenly Father has picked me up in His arms so many times...in times of sickness, and fear, and weariness, and despondency, reminding me that I will always be His child no matter how old I get, and to always come to Him as His precious child, and to trust Him as my wonderful Father.

Maybe it's something to do with finding my Heavenly Father at the grand age of thirty years, but I have been so privileged to see children come to God in their natural childlike way, and I am learning slowly...

"Thank you Abba, Father."

Chapter 12

HEALED BECAUSE JESUS STILL HEALS TODAY

And the power of the Lord was present for Him to heal the sick. Luke 5:17

JESUS STILL HEALS TODAY. That is something of which I am very confident. Indeed 'God works in mysterious ways, His wonders to perform,' as the well-known hymn goes. My confidence is accompanied by a trust in Him that there is still a mystery about the workings of God that will remain a mystery until we see Him face to face. *Then* we will see and know like we've never known.

But until then we must live by faith in the God who, in His Son, had compassion on the sick and 'healed all who came to Him'; who had compassion on the oppressed and demon possessed and set them free and healed them; who to a man who said: "If You are willing Jesus, You can heal me," replied, "I am willing. Be healed." This same Jesus saw a widow following the funeral procession of her young son. He had compassion on the woman, raised her son back to life and gave him back to his mother…healing her broken soul, and there was no greater healing for the son's body, than life from death.

The confidence of my faith in these things comes from a growing working knowledge of the Word of God. I believe the

Word no matter how things on the surface appear to contradict it or deny it. The Word remains the Truth for me even if I don't have any answers to questions like these – Why doesn't God heal everyone? Why doesn't God answer prayer? Why does He heal some and not others? Why does He heal a drunk in the street and not the loyal woman in church who does all the cleaning, arranges the flowers and attends every Sunday morning? Why does God heal that eighty-four-year-old man of cancer, but lets a three-year-old granddaughter die of leukaemia? Why? Why? Why?

We've all heard these often anguished, sometimes angry questions, and if we are honest we've probably asked some of them ourselves. But for the believer, trusting in Jesus as Lord and Saviour, we hold fast to what we *do* know about God in the Word and in our own experience, and leave the unanswered questions to Him. That's the mystery – don't fret about it. Leave it to Him. For me I am overwhelmed by the sense of His amazing compassion for this world of broken, lost, and oppressed people…both in the church and outside it. And whether or not I understand what He is or is not doing, one glance at the Cross and I know His motivation toward us all is Love…unconditional, immeasurable and incomprehensible *Love.*

My own experience of God's healing began in that YWAM mission tent in September 1977. When the sermon on 'Power to Witness' finished and the invitation was made to come to the front for those who knew they needed that Power, and were willing to surrender their lives to Jesus Christ, that's what I went forward for. I was desperate for power to witness. I had never done anything like this before. I was only used to the 1662 Prayer Book!

But I was desperate, and I was determined. I must have this power whatever the cost! And I was way out of my comfort zone…way out of my depth. But there was deep within me a rippling of excitement and anticipation. Healing was the last thing on my mind. Even though I had come into the tent in pain my focus was totally on Jesus to give me the power I needed to declare after all these months that 'Jesus is Lord,' and speak of all that He had been doing in my life for the past eighteen months. Despite the pain, healing was *not* my priority.

And what was this pain? It was something I had endured for nine years. At the age of twenty-one I was in my final year at Nonington College of Physical Education in Kent. June 1968 was summer finals, 'practicals' and written exams. The end of three years' hard slog to become a PE teacher was in sight. I was at my fittest, physically. But one afternoon after doing my athletics grades I bent down to pick up a pair of plimsolls. At the time all I felt was a slight stiffness in my lower back. A few hours later I got up from the settee when watching TV and an acute pain in my back, through my hip and down my left leg, took my breath away, and I shrieked at the shock of it. I had felt it slowly stiffening up all evening, but it was only after I had been sitting down for some time that the truth dawned – I had done something serious to my back by simply bending over to pick up a pair of plimmies.

The college doctor thought I had either sprained my back or damaged a disc. He said it couldn't be a classical slipped disc or I would be stuck in one position. What did I want to do about the rest of my finals? I was determined to finish them – I still had modern dance and gymnastics later in the next week. If I didn't finish them now I would have to come back and do my third year over again. No way was I going to do that…I was getting married in a few weeks' time, immediately after finishing college. And so my doctor gave me a supply of strong painkillers, analgesic heat rub, anti-inflammatory pills and a supply of sticky pads to tape to my lower back. And he booked me an urgent appointment with the specialist at the hospital.

I got through the rest of my finals – the motivation to do so was greater than the pain. I managed to time well all the treatment for each session, but in the evenings and trying to get up in the mornings was excruciating. But I did it – though I was also a fool. I must have done untold damage to my back. A year later I would have taken a totally different decision. I did not like teaching the sport I loved so much, to teenage girls who hated it so much. A year later I looked back and knew I would now have signed off sick, dumped my finals, cherished my back injury, got married and sorted out a job from there. Oh, the foolishness of youth!

The diagnosis of the specialist a week after I finished my finals was that I'd damaged a disc in my lumbar spine. They tried medication, different types of physiotherapy, including stretching me on the rack a number of times! Apparently it would have been easier if I had completely slipped the disc – it would have been much simpler to treat and resolve. When I moved to Ashford after the wedding my new doctor continued these efforts to resolve the damage done, but to no avail. So I was left with recurring attacks of the disc pinching outwards causing severe sciatica. Attacks averaged every six weeks and lasted for anything between five days and two weeks. The pain was excruciating. It took me ten minutes to get out of bed in the morning, and by the time I got to the bathroom and looked in the mirror my face was totally grey with sweat pouring down it. I never knew what triggered off an attack, and I never knew when it would burn out and subside, leaving me with a stiffness that was always threatening the next attack. My doctor gave up with it and simply prescribed two lots of powerful painkillers for me to collect whenever an attack started. Seven years went by. Nothing changed. I lived with it, and thought I had it for life. Little did I know that Someone greater than me had other ideas!

My dad was visiting in 1975 and offered to fund me a course at an osteopath; he'd heard good reports on people with sport's injuries. I made some enquiries and decided to take him up on his offer. I had a course of ten treatments, and what a difference they made. My back felt much 'safer' and the recurring attacks stopped. It felt like I had a new life…but it didn't last. Six months passed and I started to feel familiar twinges of pain. Another six months and the attacks were back in full force. I put up with them. An osteopath was expensive; I couldn't afford to pay for more treatment and I didn't like to ask my dad again. Two months later my dad was dead and God broke into my life.

Eighteen months later yet another attack began the day before I was intending to go to the YWAM tent meeting. My dad had bequeathed the whole of his estate between my sister and myself so I had some cash in the bank and I decided to treat myself to another course with the osteopath that I'd previously visited in Folkestone. I knew my dad would have considered that a good use of some of the money he had left me. So that morning I rang up and made an appointment for my first treatment later that week.

Later that day my minister picked me up and took me to the tent meeting…the one I went to two days after my conversion to Jesus Christ, as I have recorded in chapter six.

When I went forward for power to witness I was waiting a long time before Julius, the Nigerian, came and ministered to me. What I want to share now is the amazing thing that happened as I waited. I stood with my eyes closed and enjoyed the atmosphere; I can't say I put too much in the way of prayer together, but I was praying inside, and peace settled in my heart. I felt a touch from behind. Someone was placing both their hands on my back – one hand on my lower back, the other in the middle. I flinched, *not* out of fear or surprise, but in response to the power of the touch. I had no idea who it was, and I didn't feel I needed to. Immediately that someone behind me started to speak to God; I recognised the rich tone and accent of a black African woman. I listened and I didn't hear her praying for me. Instead she was simply praising and thanking God. This stranger kept her hands on my back and got on with her worship and adoration of God. Power surged through my whole body; it took my breath away. It felt like my lungs were being filled with fresh mountain air. I just let it happen. I have explained it inadequately, but God was at work, and He was doing a whole lot more than I could ever explain. All I know is that I didn't want it to stop. But it did. The woman stopped speaking and gently lifted her hands from my body. I stood still, kept my eyes closed and kept drinking it all in. I never turned round to see the woman. I never met her at all. She was just a servant of God being obedient to Him, and I got blessed and He gets all the Glory. Hallelujah!

It was just a few minutes later that Julius came up and asked if I wanted prayer…

At the end of the meeting I made my way back from the front to the very back of the tent where my minister was still sitting. I hugged a number of total strangers on the way, and finished up by giving him a big hug too! I noticed as I walked that my back felt loose, and as we drove back in the car there was no stiffness or pain. I wondered...

I woke up next morning, and gingerly started to roll out of bed onto one knee as I had done so many times during the past nine years. But I realised there was *no* pain. I got up, dressed and went downstairs – all these movements would have been so painful with the onset of a fresh attack, which had begun the day before. I was now on very unfamiliar ground. Could this possibly be real? By the end of the afternoon I was convinced; the looseness in my back that I had felt when in the tent was still loose! One thing anyone who has had similar back trouble will know, is that even during the times when the back is behaving itself, there is a residual stiffness remaining, always threatening another attack sooner or later. That stiffness had gone! I was healed, and I knew it. After all these years I was healed, and God had done it the evening before when He must have given that African lady a Word of Knowledge so that she knew where to lay her hands and she knew what God was doing when she did her part, and all she could do was praise Him. *She knew!* That's why all she did was praise and thank Him.

I learned a huge lesson from God that evening, right at the beginning of my Christian life. I listened to the teaching in the sermon saying – Don't seek tongues, it's not a toy; seek power to witness. So I asked for power to witness and with it God gave me the gift of tongues, as a beautiful liberating prayer language! Also, even though I was in pain, I didn't ask for healing because I was totally focussed on receiving power to witness. So God again took me by surprise and healed me. What a God! What Love! And it was all directed at me!

But as a result of God's work in my life right at the beginning *I knew* that I was His child; *I knew* Him and His amazing Love; *I knew* I was born again of the Spirit, filled with the Holy Spirit and had been given a love for the Word of God. The next day when I opened my Bible and started reading it aloud the gift of tongues came pouring out of my mouth. That happened a number of times in the early days! So I had my nose in the Bible every day and I prayed in tongues daily too. *I knew* I had power to witness and so I started witnessing to people straightaway. *I knew* that Jesus still healed today, so I knew I could start praying for people to be healed and expect to see answers; and *I knew* from the example of the lady praying for me, that God could use me also to bring healing into people's lives. And I believed obedience was the key to that.

Over these thirty years since that night, I have received healing many times…physical, emotional, spiritual. Sometimes it has been just me and God, having a breakthrough with Him alone. At other times I have gone forward publicly for prayer or asked for it in a prayer meeting or house group…sometimes with laying on of hands, sometimes without. And there have been times when God has spoken to someone miles away to pray for me, and I have been touched by God at just the right moment and known what He has done. And I have said to Him: "Did you ask someone to pray just then?" And if He brings someone immediately to mind, I have contacted that person and asked him or her if God impressed upon him or her to pray for me. And what encouragement there is to both of us when he or she replies in the affirmative and pinpoints the time God spoke to him/her, and it was the same time that I had registered and kept in my own heart! And then that is a testimony to encourage the body.

These were special times in the very cold winter of 1996. Diagnosed with unstable angina in the January, I was on a long waiting list until October to have an angiogram at Guy's Hospital. There were a number of times that I thought 'This is it,' but it wasn't.

My doctor said: "If you have a problem, don't call me, go straight to A and E."

A couple of years later he admitted that it was a miracle that I didn't have a heart attack during that time. I reminded him (I had witnessed to him throughout the crisis period) that God was into miracles and He wanted me around a bit longer as there were things still for me to do! The whole period was like living on a precipice, but it was one of the most significant growing times for my faith that I have ever experienced.

Right at the beginning of the New Year, 1996, the Spirit of God gave me a Scripture that I believe became a 'lifesaver' to me. It was Psalm 118:17 and I declared it daily…many times a day, whenever He brought it to mind –

> *"I will not die but live and will proclaim the mighty works of God."*

That Word was *Life* to me with a capital "L". And it also became a powerful prophetic Word in my life for I did *not* die; I lived to proclaim the mighty works of God at home and in other lands such as Russia, America, Israel.

And it was during this winter, too, that He regularly called people to pray for me out of the blue, and I believed this thwarted the devil's tactics. *He* wanted me dead before it was my time.

Despite the severity of the winter cold and the angina, I still never gave up taking the dog for a walk. These daily walks through local fields and woods had always been amazing times of fellowship with Jesus, and it would take another book to recall and record the times I had with Him whilst my Springer Spaniel, Boris, exercised himself, in the exuberant way that particular breed does!

Only once that winter did I only get to the top of the road before half collapsing on someone's wall because there was no oxygen getting from my heart to my lungs. I managed to struggle back in the house and was in bed for the rest of the day feeling very unwell.

But on other occasions when the frost was thick and white I went out as usual with a woollen hat and thick scarf wrapped around my face to stop the cold air getting to my lungs. I would get so far around the walk and sometimes lose my breath. I resisted (just about) the rising panic that would have got me running for home, because I know I would never have got there if I'd done that. I would focus on Jesus and take very deliberate small steps to combat the panic and breathlessness. Out of the blue I would be surprised by a sense of peace followed by joy. That's when I sensed He had called someone to pray. And when I followed that up it was true…He had. Such memories of Him are so sweet.

There was an occasion in early spring, when the weather was warmer and the sun was out, that He clearly spoke to me:

"Sue, which would be your choice, for Me to take you home to Glory, or for Me to heal you?" I pondered that for a few moments and answered:

"Lord, You know my heart. My answer is 'both'. I know I am going to be with You in Glory, but if I ask You to take me now that will be for my benefit and blessing only. But if You heal me I will be the first to be blessed, and You will be able to bless others through me as I share Jesus with them. I want as many years as You want to give me, to touch as many lives as I can for You before I go Home to Glory with You."

"You have answered well, Sue."

"Thank you Lord. It was a good question!"

I eventually had the angiogram and it showed that all my coronary arteries were blocked almost totally and high up in the widest part of the descending arteries. The good news medically was they were so high that angioplasty was possible on all of them rather than opening up my chest for a triple bypass. The not so good news was that if I'd had a heart attack on any one of them, then one third of my heart would have been severely damaged, and the chances are it would have killed me. It was serious enough to bring me back into hospital in a couple of weeks and have angioplasty on two of the arteries. The surgeon wouldn't do all three in one go because he'd never done three before and he reckoned it would put too much strain on my heart! So he said he would have me back in four weeks and do the third just before Christmas. An appointment would be sent to me.

Christmas came and went and no appointment came. I wasn't particularly concerned about another visit to the hospital just yet as I had gone down with a nasty chest infection, and it took until the end of January 1997 to clear up. Feeling better, I contacted Guy's Hospital to enquire about the delay. I was told I wasn't on a waiting list for treatment! I rang my surgeon's secretary and she followed it up for me. One morning I arrived in from my one-hour's work as a 'sniffer' at Quest to find Peter with a furrowed brow and looking very concerned. He had taken a phone call from Guy's Hospital to say that, because there were insufficient funds from our Health Trust, Guy's were not treating any more patients from our trust until the new financial year. I would be sent an appointment after May 1st.

Everyone concerned was horrified, especially as I was not a *new* patient, and already in the middle of treatment. They could do nothing about it and were extremely sorry. Peter had written these details down and invited me to read the message. As I did an inexplicable thing happened. I had a rush of joy rise up from deep within me and I giggled. I managed to stem the tide of it for Peter's sake. Certainly on the surface there wasn't anything to laugh about and he asked:

"What are you laughing about?"

"I don't know," I replied. "I'll just take the dog for a walk now."

I put my coat, hat, and boots on quickly, and got the lead on Boris our Springer spaniel, and off we went up the road and into the woods and fields that were our regular haunt. Boris set off at a sprint as he normally did to explore every bush and tree and rabbit hole as if there was no tomorrow. I went at a much more leisurely pace so as not to aggravate the angina. I still had one artery to be cleared.

I was aiming for my favourite field, which was surrounded by high hedges and was very secluded. I went in there for special times with the Lord. And this was a special time. The joy was rippling around inside me and I walked along praying in tongues, simply enjoying the fellowship with Jesus.

Once I got into this field I asked Him:

"Jesus, what was all that about when I read that message? What is it You want to say to me?"

His answer was immediate and one of those very occasional times when it sounds audible:

"There may be insufficient funds for your treatment, but I have paid in full for your healing!"

Wow! My heart overflowed in love and praise. This was one of those precious moments when time seems to stop still as I enjoyed the embrace of the One who loves me so much, the One I fell in love with twenty years before. It was as though His Spirit nudged me when I read that awful message from Guy's Hospital and He was saying:

"Come away with Me, come now." I repeated His words back to Him:

"There may be insufficient funds for your treatment, but I have paid in full for your healing!"

"Jesus, how I needed to hear you say that. How I love You for loving me so much."

I had the third angioplasty on the fourteenth of May 1997, four days after celebrating my fiftieth birthday! The artery was 100% blocked, but I had come a long way in trusting God that my days were numbered in *His* book and nobody else's!

Six months later I had a check up at the hospital. A nurse friend warned me that the doctor I was to see was an atheist and a bit aggressive. The doctor was looking at me as I walked into the room. I said a cheery 'Good afternoon,' and she beckoned me to sit down. She perused my notes…quite a thick wadge they were by now!

Then she spoke: "Well, you don't *look* sick."

"What do you mean?" I asked.

"I watched you walk in, and your whole demeanour, the way you walked, and the happy look on your face doesn't speak to me of a person that has gone through what I read here in your notes!"

I thought for a second that maybe, if she is an aggressive atheist, perhaps she is setting me up for a put down. But putting that aside I responded in the only way I could think to do so.

"Having Jesus in my life has made all the difference to the way I've lived through it all."

"You are a Christian then?"

"Yes."

"Well, you are certainly looking very well on it!"

"Thank you."

She then dismissed me.

She could see healing in my face. She certainly didn't respond aggressively when I gave credit to Jesus for what she saw. I am no evangelist, but I am, as a Christian, a witness, and I love such opportunities to give Jesus the credit. For me to keep silent is not an option. The Glory *must* go to God. Praise Him.

Chapter 13

BRANCHES BEAR FRUIT

Abide in Me, and I in you. As the branch cannot bear fruit of itself, unless it abides in the vine, neither can you, unless you abide in Me. John 15:4 (NKJ)

JENNIFER.
It was just a few weeks after my conversion that I met Jennifer. I had been going to the Bible Study and we were asked by the curate to pray for a Jennifer whom he'd never met, but who had rung him asking about services and sharing enough about herself to make him a little concerned. Despite a lack of experience of praying aloud I felt greatly urged to do so.

A week or so later she arrived at a service and I was introduced to her. I sensed God at work here, and the next week she came to both services, morning and evening, and stayed for a cuppa and a chat afterwards. Here she spoke briefly to say she had just started coming back to church after a ten-year absence. She seemed tense and a little nervous – a bit daunted at taking the plunge again, I thought. But I wondered whether she knew Jesus. Was she just coming back to the church or was she also coming back to Him?

She wasn't in church the next week. Then about ten days later, whilst Peter and I were eating lunch, I was struck by an urgency to contact her. The Lord was telling me to phone her *now*! So strong was the urge that I excused myself and got up in the middle of the meal to phone her. I had no idea what I was supposed to be ringing her about. Help, Lord! As soon as Jennifer spoke I could tell she was in deep trouble. She could hardly control her voice, and I realised I must be careful what I said. In fact, it would be better if she did the talking! She was taken aback to get my call out of the blue; but after a little hesitation she decided to tell me what the trouble was. She explained that she had had a serious nervous breakdown, and had already spent several months off work – she was a medical secretary at a local hospital. I remember little of what I said to her but I just wanted to comfort her and strengthen her, and help her feel a little better for having shared. She was much calmer by the end of the call; I asked her if she would like me to call on her one afternoon, and she said yes and thanked me for calling. I also gave her my phone number if she felt she needed to ring and have a chat.

A few days later I visited her at her home. She seemed quite cheerful, and pleased to see me. But I still felt in the dark. She then told me that at the time I phoned her out of the blue she had reached her lowest point. It felt like the darkest ever moment of her life and that she would never surface from it. She was having suicidal thoughts. Then the phone rang and the few words I spoke were enough to pull her back from the point of no return. I could hardly contain my feelings as I told her the Lord had told me to phone in that moment. It was as though sunshine broke out across her face. Something broke in her life as she realised how much God must care for her. What a wonderful thing it was to observe. What a patient and gracious God; we enjoyed fellowship with Him as we sat there praising Him together. We both were strengthened in our faith, and a bond was, that day, formed between us by the Holy Spirit.

I learned a sober lesson for the first time with Jennifer – the importance of obeying God no matter how strange it may seem. There are consequences of obeying God and there are consequences of not obeying God. The consequences of not obeying His voice to ring Jennifer immediately that day do not bear thinking about. There have been instances in ensuing years when I didn't obey His voice and regretted it terribly, and I want to thank God for His gracious patience and endurance with me as I've been really slow to learn some of these lessons, despite that early encounter with Jennifer.

DONNA.
I met Donna around Christmas '79 at a Tuesday morning fellowship – a quiet, shy, tense young mum about my age. She was new to Ashford and had moved onto the new Highfield Estate with her husband Frank and two children. She started to attend regularly and despite her shyness seemed hungry spiritually. One day, on leaving the meeting, Donna remarked to another member of the fellowship: "I don't think I'll ever be like Sue and Jane!" Jane was my prayer partner.

I felt a mixed reaction to that remark. What did she mean? Was she attracted to our faith…or put off by it? I felt a mixture of excitement, challenge and concern. I didn't want people looking at me, but at Jesus. I didn't want Donna looking at my faith and comparing it to hers, and feeling she didn't measure up. So I prayed urgently – help, Lord! And He did. He opened my eyes a little further and showed me a much healthier reaction to her remark. He showed me that Donna was longing for a relationship with Him that she saw in us. And He assured me that was how it should be…that was good. So I put it into prayer: "Lord Jesus, if Donna feels a big difference between us, then the only thing that makes that difference is our relationship with You. Lord, I want her to have the same intimate relationship with You that I have."

Having prayed, my burden for Donna grew. I planned to visit her and talk to her – several times, in fact! But it never worked out. It dawned on me, oh so slowly, that the Holy Spirit was gently restraining me. So I went back to prayer and asked God to give me some specific direction on how He wanted me to pray. And He did. He gave me three things to focus on in prayer: – First, that she would experience the presence of the Lord; then, that she would have a real assurance of salvation; and thirdly, that she would be filled with the Holy Spirit.

During the prayer time in the next Tuesday afternoon Fellowship, Donna prayed like I'd never heard her pray before. She was so quiet I heard only some words, but clearly she was opening her heart to the Lord. It was electric…the presence of the Lord was overwhelming. God was doing His own business with her, and once again I felt restrained by His Spirit, and I held back from laying hands on her and praying. I discovered when the meeting broke up that I wasn't the only one to have the same experience. God didn't want us pre-empting Him, and we knew His timing was always perfect. So there was an excitement and anticipation running through the group.

It was a fortnight before we met again. The meeting was good but quiet and uneventful. As we were leaving Donna hesitated by my car, changed her mind, and hurriedly crossed the road. Her home was just a short walk away. Julia, whose house we met in, whispered:

"Call her back. I think it may be important." So I did. Donna came back and rushed out:

"I've wanted to speak to you for two weeks," she said. "It may sound silly, because I'm not sure what about. It's just that I'm sure I've got to come and see you!"

My heart started to thump. Now *this* was God's timing, but I wasn't sure what about either, but I was certainly excited!

We arranged to meet for coffee a couple of mornings later. She arrived right on time, but very nervous. She started to share at my invitation. I felt a growing empathy with her as I remembered from my own experience this great need and desire to talk about God in a personal way, which had come for me when I met Jesus. But it had at first felt quite difficult to do – shyness, embarrassment, self-consciousness, and fear of rejection all rolled into one. The Lord had released me so much in this, and I recognised Donna's need. As she talked I clearly saw the Lord's hand on her. So strong had been the lead to come, and so fierce was her hunger and desire to know more of Him that she had battled with the shyness and fear with great determination. Nothing was going to stop her. My heart was already singing – "Hallelujah, for the Lord our God the Almighty reigns!"

Donna shared that a fortnight ago in the House Group she had been overwhelmed by the presence of the Lord. She had prayed but didn't know what to do next. Then things started to become clear to her, started to drop into place. She realised that although she had always called herself a Christian she didn't have a personal relationship with Jesus as Saviour, and she had never actually asked Him into her life to take control.

So she went straight home from that meeting and before getting ready for bed had got down on her knees and asked Jesus to come into her life. That was just the beginning. She was immediately given a hunger for more. She guessed that that may have something to do with the Holy Spirit but understood very little about Him. She remembered that somewhere the Bible promised His fullness, and even commanded believers to be filled with the Holy Spirit. That must be what she needed, and that was why she had come today. She wanted to know more.

I gulped. I had not been in this position before. I was out of my depth, but I knew God was not out of His! What a lovely experience it was to 'let go and let God!' I realised He had had all this planned down to the smallest detail. We chatted as I opened up the Bible verses relevant to the situation. I relaxed more and more as He used me to minister His Word into Donna's life. How I loved doing that. What a privilege. He had released her to share like she'd never done before, and in this way brought healing in her life. As she warmed to His Presence and gentle guiding, she visibly relaxed too.

The talking over, she wanted prayer. She wanted Jesus to baptise her in His Holy Spirit. I threw up a quick prayer:

"What now, Lord?"

I knew instinctively there was no need to delay. We had a time of prayer, confession, praise and worship. By then I believe the Holy Spirit had already come down upon Donna…upon both of us, in fact. His Presence was so real and we were quietly bathing in Him. I slipped onto my knees before Donna, laid my hands on her, and asked Jesus to baptise her in the Holy Spirit, and we both thanked Him for doing so. We prayed together again during which time the Lord gave me a Word for Donna:

"The gift has been given for you to appropriate when you are ready."

I left her to pray alone. As I got on quietly making a cup of coffee in the kitchen, I heard Donna start to sing. When I returned she wasn't singing quietly anymore! She was just bursting out in song – she just had to give outlet in praise as she began to overflow. I was momentarily amused and stifled a giggle, because to my knowledge Donna couldn't sing in tune, and would normally have avoided trying to do so. But of course singing in the Spirit is something quite different and in Donna' case – a miracle! Anyway, with joy bubbling in my heart I joined in and we sang together praising the Lord. I stopped once to see what she would do, but there was no stopping her. She just continued praising God, giving outlet to the Holy Spirit, and He gave her a new voice!

She left my house at 1 p.m. that day knowing that she had met with God in a new way and would never be the same again!

Four months later and Donna was going from strength to strength. There were areas in her life where she wanted to be released to worship and witness with boldness and freedom. Since being filled with the Holy Spirit she had had a longing for a further release of her tongue. In retrospect by this time I had realised that the Word the Lord gave – "The gift has been given for you to appropriate when you are ready" – was referring to the gift of tongues.

Jane and I invited Donna to join us for prayer. We had been prayer partners for about two years, and had grown rapidly as believers as a result of meeting once a week to pray. We were so blessed that we covenanted together with God to give away something of what we were receiving from Him so that others could be blessed too. He led us to invite Donna to join us. During our time together one Friday morning I had a picture of a dam with the hand visible of someone about halfway up the dam wall – a very precarious position! The hand was carefully scratching away at the wall, trying to make a very small hole in the wall to let out a small amount of water that was behind the dam. It looked a ridiculous thing to be doing. The person was trying to control the flow, wanting some, not all. But I realised that as soon as a break started to form in the wall there would be no stopping the water. The hole would get larger and eventually would crack the wall and break through in a rushing torrent, carrying everything with it that was on the other side.

As I meditated on this God showed me this was Donna. She wanted total release to praise the Lord but still had some fears about the power of the Holy Spirit overwhelming her. So she was creeping slowly forward with God trying to control her fear by controlling the flow! Lord, what are you going to do? I kept quiet about the picture.

When our prayer time had finished Donna said she had felt a 'funny' feeling in her throat like a lump that made her voice sound husky. (I silently smiled!) She had wanted to let go in praise and let Him give her the words! She believed she had been given the gift of tongues when she had been filled with the Holy Spirit that morning she spent with me, but she had held back then and had the same feeling in her throat! Each time this happened she had a strong desire to speak out in an unknown language, but didn't and she believed this was fear. I briefly shared the picture I had had and then we left. When I stopped the car outside her house I asked her two questions – Do you want to speak in tongues? YES. Does God want you to speak in tongues? YES. Without further comment I left.

Jane and I met again for serious prayer about this. For the first time we pleaded the power of the Blood of Jesus over the situation and knew His Peace. We felt it was 'job done'.

A couple of afternoons later I knocked on Donna's door. She was pleased to see me, seemed very relaxed and we had a good time of fellowship. Then out of the blue she said:

"I think I prayed in tongues on Wednesday." The first thing that struck me with amusement was her modesty with the understatement of: "I think…"

Something obviously had happened to her and she *knew* it. She then shared what had happened. She'd had coffee that morning with another Christian from the House Group, and their sharing together galvanised her faith again. She went home determined to take a step of faith with God. After lunch and Frank had gone back to work, she got on her knees to do business with God. She told Him she wanted to take a step of faith…more of a plunge, really! She wanted to praise Him with real freedom; she wanted the gift of tongues to do so; she believed He wanted her to be free and had already given her the gift. Then, having said her piece, she waited…and waited. Nothing happened.

Eventually she got up thinking – 'Well, that's that then.' She put on a record her friend had lent her that morning…the same morning Jane and I had prayed and believed – 'job done'! So Donna sat back in an easy chair and relaxed as she enjoyed listening to the music. She was listening to the words of a lovely song – "…descend sweet gentle dove…" She closed her eyes and started humming to it. She didn't know the words; it was a new song written by a singer from a local church.

Suddenly she shot bolt upright! She didn't know the words – the English words, that is. But she was certainly putting words to it. She flew onto her knees and just let them come, in prayer and praise to God. The words of an unknown language came in a torrent. The dam had burst! And she felt the Peace of the Lord come down upon her and overwhelm her in a mighty way. She put two hands on her head and said to me:

"It really felt as though the gentle dove of the Holy Spirit was resting on my head, just like this!"

Her face shone as she shared. She was reluctant to get up; she wanted to stay on her knees praising God in this new way, but she suddenly realised the children were due to be collected from school! She threw on her coat and rushed up the road, still praising God. It just kept pouring out of her mouth! She put her hand over her mouth in case the neighbours thought she was mad! But still it kept coming.

As she neared the school gates she was struck with momentary horror. She always met three or four other mums in the playground for a chat. She usually talked very quickly anyway, but what if she opened her mouth and the flow continued, and she couldn't say what she intended to say? As she shared this with me we both rolled over with laughter. Of course it worked out fine. When she met her fellow mums she spoke quite normally in English. This was all so new to her and very exciting, but she learned another lesson about our wonderful and gracious God – the gift of tongues is from Him, but we are in control of it. We can choose to use it or not, and we can choose when to start and when to stop praying in tongues. He never forces Himself upon us, and always leaves us with the freedom to choose. And that is the nature of real Love. Donna and I finished with a time of joyful worship, thanking Him for His wonderful sense of humour!

Chapter 14

THE ENEMY IS CLOSER THAN YOU THINK

Be sober; be vigilant; because your adversary the devil walks about like a roaring lion, seeking whom he may devour. Resist him, steadfast in the faith... 1Peter 5:8 (NKJ)

THEORETICALLY I think I believed in the existence of the devil because of my religious upbringing. But mental assent was as far as that went; I believed what I had been taught but I had no awareness of his *personal* nature. Little did I know it but I was in for some surprises! I've been in many evangelical meetings in the past thirty years, and in a few...not many, the invitation has been something like this – 'Come to Jesus, say this prayer after me asking Jesus into your heart to cleanse you from your sins and you will be saved. When you become a Christian your life will change, and all your problems will disappear.' Don't misunderstand me here. I have no problem with leading someone to Christ this way and leading them in a prayer of good confession. But trying to draw people with a carrot like 'all your problems will be over when Jesus comes into your heart' is unfair, not godly, and unbiblical. It just isn't true. In fact, the opposite is true. You will get rid of some of your old problems when you are born again, but you

111

will discover a whole lot of new ones when you become a follower of Jesus Christ.

My personal experience was simply this – when Jesus became a real person to me, then the devil became a real person too. Why is this? Well, I came by new birth into the spiritual realm. Up until then I lived my life in the realm of my body and soul; my spirit existed deep inside me in the dark and was effectively dead because of sin. The light was switched on in my spirit when Jesus, the Light of the world, came in and took up residence by His Spirit, the Holy Spirit, and my spirit came alive. Jesus said: *"No one can see [enter] the Kingdom of God unless he is born again [of the Spirit]."John 3:3.* The spiritual realm became real to me for the first time as I entered the Kingdom of God.

I discovered very quickly that I now had spiritual eyes and spiritual ears. I was acutely aware of this realm for the first time in my life. I knew that I knew that I knew! But the spiritual realm is divided into two – good and evil, light and darkness, God and Satan. Be assured these are *not* equal kingdoms with equal rulers with equal power. Jesus is King of Kings and Lord of Lords, and He reigns over *all.* Satan is a fallen angel, a created being. Pride comes before a fall and he fell big time from Heaven because of his pride. And he took a whole load of rebellious angels with him. The Scripture above says he goes about like a roaring lion. The clue word is *'like'.* He is a usurper and a deceiver and if he can con us into believing he *is* a roaring lion, he will, and we will be frightened of him. There is only one lion and He is the Lion of Judah, and His Name is Jesus, and even Satan must bow the knee to Him; but there's no way he wants you to know that!

From the very start of my new life in Christ I was aware that I had an enemy who hated me, and would try everything to destroy me and my new faith in Jesus. In chapter nine I shared about waking up suddenly before dawn the morning after my conversion and baptism in the Holy Spirit. I felt icy cold. Death was in the air; I'd felt the same coldness the night my dad died. A voice spoke to me:

"What have you done? Stop it now before you go too far and wont be able to get back."

I'd not heard this voice before, but I knew who it was. I now had the Holy Spirit in me giving me discernment, and this was the first lesson of many in the discipleship school of the Spirit of Jesus. I was an enlisted soldier being trained for the army of the Lord. And God wasn't hanging around! I realised this wouldn't be the last time that the devil or any of his fallen angels, called demons, would speak to me, so I might as well start off as I meant to go on. I replied:

"Be quiet. I won't listen to you. I belong to Jesus now. Be quiet in Jesus' Name!" The coldness went, the Peace of God settled in the room, dawn broke and the sun came up, and joy filled my soul!

With this realisation that we do have an enemy who is real I also realised at this time that it was *not* my first encounter with him, but my second. The first was the night my dad died and the tug-o'-war that I was having as I prayed, pulling my dad through a prickly hedge against an unseen foe. Yes, it was the same coldness and the same adversary.

Over the following years there were many lessons, tailor-made for me, in God's training school for disciples, training me to be a soldier in the Lord's army. The most important lesson – *know your enemy.* How? Well, there are do's and there are don'ts. *Don't* spend a load of time studying Satan and his works and the work of his forces of unclean spirits. He loves that sort of attention, because it gets your eyes off Jesus, the Author and Finisher of your faith. Instead, *do* spend lots of time in the Word of God, the Scriptures, until you begin to think scripturally and understand people and life's events from a Scriptural point of view. As you do these, allow the Holy Spirit to be your teacher, so that you understand by discernment the things of God, and recognise when things aren't of God.

I remember very well an illustration of this principle, when I read an article that came my way at just the right time. It spoke of a time in the USA when newly employed bank tellers were trained in the basement of the bank wearing blindfolds. The job required that they were confident in recognising any counterfeit note that passed through their hands. Were they trained on counterfeit notes? Not at all. They were trained to handle only genuine dollar bills. They were trained to feel the real thing and recognise it. Hence the use of blindfolds. They were only fit to go upstairs and take up their position at the bank counter once they were so good at knowing the feel of the genuine article that they would know instinctively when a counterfeit note was placed in their hands. And it is the same with Christians – we are to spend time getting to know the Truth intimately, and then we will be confident in recognising when and where the enemy is at work, without wasting precious time looking for him. This is God's equipping for Kingdom ministry. I wonder how many believers are so equipped for God to use. I discovered that many believers, including myself, were ill-equipped to be used by God in pastoral and deliverance ministry. As I had been, many are still oppressed by the enemy themselves, to a lesser or greater degree. Because of ignorance, and unbelief that the enemy *can* maintain a legal right to an area of one's life, they remain in bondage instead of enjoying the full freedom of belonging to

Jesus Christ, and are unable effectively to help other brethren or sisters they see in desperate need.

"For we do not wrestle against flesh and blood, but against principalities, against powers, against the rulers of the darkness of this age, against spiritual hosts of wickedness in the heavenly places." Ephesians 6:12 NKJ. Paul's words here are clear directions that when under attack, don't fight the person – pray for them. In prayer bring down the spiritual forces driving them, using weapons that are spiritual for the bringing down of strongholds.

With God the teaching wasn't all theory. I began to recognise the spiritual in people, learning to discern between the Holy Spirit and unclean spirits. In the early days there were some quite hairy experiences. I had a choice…run…or stay! Choosing to stay put me on a steep learning curve with God. Only staying and learning from Him brought Glory to God, and His help to those in need. I have picked out just two situations to share here, and later my own experience of God delivering me from the bondage that the enemy was desperate to hold me in.

It was Christmas 1981. I had been a Christian for just over four years and what an adventure it had been so far! I received a letter from Lyndsey Ingles that filled me with such joy and gratitude to the Lord for seeing her through to a safe haven. With her letter in my hand, I sat in the easy chair and looked back with Him to what I had known of her.

It must have been sometime in the winter of 1979 when I met her at an evening service. She sat in the pew behind me and was quick to chat when I turned around at the end of the service. In no time she was into spiritual things, eager to talk. I wasn't getting that witness in my spirit so I asked her how long she had been a Christian and was taken aback by her answer – on and off for several years. How can you be a Christian 'on and off', I thought? Still, she was open and keen to talk, mentioning such things as baptism in the Holy Spirit, speaking in tongues, the previous fellowship she had been in, and the fact that she had sung in The Witness.

The more we talked the more uneasy I became – a deep uneasiness I felt, but so strong. What on earth was it? I saw her several times after that, usually in church. There was something about her that was just not right. She seemed quite a tense person; at times she was eager to chat and share, at others quite evasive. She shared a little of her home background in Scotland. She hadn't been happy; she'd started seeking the Lord; someone ministered to her and persuaded her to be confirmed. But had she been converted? Was it that? I don't know, but the uneasiness in my spirit continued.

There *was* something missing in her life and experience – there was no joy for a start – almost the opposite, in fact. She was not a happy person. She needed the Lord; she knew it too. She had decided to be confirmed; had her desperate needs been met there? Had any problems in relationships, starting with her parents, been healed? Was she feeling in a worse state than when she started? She'd certainly been honest about coming down to Kent to get as far away from home and family as possible. To be honest I would have preferred to have avoided her. I felt uncomfortable in her presence. There was something drastically wrong spiritually. And did I really want to know?

The news came like a thunderbolt out of the blue. Lyndsey was in hospital after taking an overdose. I then discovered she had tried to take her own life on several previous occasions. Fortunately she had not succeeded – but what if she had? I felt sick. Where did all this fit in with her seeking the Lord, running from home, being a Christian, singing in The Witness, and obviously seeking Christian fellowship? For all these things were apparently part of Lyndsey's make-up. I came up with an answer – spiritual warfare. Things didn't add up; her life was a mess and Satan intended keeping it that way. He would be angry to lose her to Jesus, and would be bent on her destruction, the sooner the better. God was beginning to put some of the theory into practice. Fieldwork was going to be a much less comfortable experience than the schoolroom!

Mindful that Jesus sent His disciples out in twos I asked my prayer partner, Jane, if she would go with me to visit Lyndsey in the hospital. And so off we went one evening after praying together. Lyndsey was obviously very moved that we'd bothered to come, that someone seemed to care. I sensed her utter loneliness and fear. She wanted us there but she seemed uncomfortable. I felt uneasy again in her presence and sensed that she was in a tug-o-war. I looked at Jane and knew we were in the same place. I threw up a quick prayer for help from the Lord, and He immediately gave me understanding. The enemy cannot stand the presence of the Holy Spirit, and there was a real sense of opposing forces in that room. How much Lyndsey understood I don't know, but she certainly couldn't cope with what was being stirred up. And it was the Holy Spirit in Jane and myself who was disturbing the enemy. Either we backed off and left or we faced it out.

Lyndsey would swing from sheer delight that we had come, and then suddenly there would be a look of helpless desolation and fear in her face. I didn't understand why she should try to take her own life, but I had a glimpse of the evil power that might push her to the edge.

At this stage in our Christian experience the only thing we knew to do was to pray.

"Would you like us to pray with you before we go, Lyndsey?"

"Yes please," she replied, with a pleading look in her eyes speaking a silent "Help me." As we prayed there was a tremendous sense of rising tension in the room, of her closing off completely. Probably against her will, I thought. Something or someone was messing with her mind. We left feeling sober, sad, and helpless. What on earth were we up against? And more important – what was Lyndsey up against? I felt really angry...

The next news we had was of Lyndsey's transfer to St Augustine's Psychiatric Hospital for further treatment. On discovering it was her birthday in a few days' time the Fellowship Group that she had joined at our home decided to surprise her, to remind her that there were people outside who were still thinking of her and praying for her. And so on a beautiful warm May afternoon, that was Lyndsey's birthday, I drove over to the hospital at Chartham, in the middle of the country between Ashford and Canterbury. I went armed with cards, presents, good wishes, and even a birthday cake from the group. To be honest I went with some trepidation, as I'd never been in a mental hospital before. This was another first – God was really beginning to stretch me! Once more my comfort zone was being breached, and I felt out of my depth. Looking back now I realise this has been the story of my life with Jesus!

But this day it was worth it to see the look on Lyndsey's face. She was surprised and delighted at my arrival. She said that just a visit would have been more than enough to make her day! But the armful of birthday goodies too...she felt overwhelmed. She'd never been treated like this before. Why did people care so much for her? I told her it was because Jesus wanted her to know how much He loved her and was using people who love Him to show her!

We talked and we walked. The grounds of the hospital were beautiful and she took me on a tour of some of them. When it was time to say goodbye in the car park, she made the first response of its kind that I'd seen her make...she'd always been so tense and tight. She gave me an impulsive hug, and tried to express her thanks. It was my turn to be surprised and overwhelmed. To me it was a big ray of hope in what can feel like a hopeless place to both patients and their visitors. I drove slowly down the long tree-lined drive with my eyes blurred with tears.

The next time I saw Lyndsey the circumstances were quite different. She was still in St Augustine's but had made another attempt at suicide whilst in there. I was stunned at the news. How is it possible in a place like that? I thought she was safe! But I suppose that if anyone is determined enough they'll find a way. My visit this time was not a happy affair. Lyndsey was pleased to see me but much quieter in herself...much more subdued. I suspected she was on some powerful medication. Once again it was a lovely sunny day but there was no walking out in the beautiful grounds this time. Because of her latest attempt she was in a locked ward and under close observation.

Because the staff knew me from the last visit they made a concession. We were led to a room so that we could have some privacy from the other patients. The door was closed and we were told the member of staff would be outside if we needed them. The room was a large, bare sitting room, furnished with just a few chairs. The sun streamed through the large bay window but it didn't feel sunny in there. The emptiness of the room just heightened the deeper emptiness that was her life. We talked. She was glad to...she had begun to trust me. She obviously needed to talk but found it difficult. It was as though she was switching on and off – one minute here, the next minute somewhere else. I wondered how much of what she was saying was true and how much was not. Was she aware of the difference? I sensed a spirit of deception at work. I felt helpless and desperately sad for her. Again I felt the presence of the enemy, but this time just sitting there looking me in the eye, mocking. Lyndsey had no fight in her; she didn't seem to care about anything any more. She said her parents were visiting in a few days, coming down from Scotland to see her. That distressed her; if she could possibly avoid that, she would.

One ray of hope she had was a suggestion from a member of staff who was a Christian that there was the possibility of transferring her to a Christian treatment centre in Brentwood, Essex. It was only a vague suggestion at this stage. A lot depended on how she responded to her treatment here and the recommendation of her doctor if he thought it would be appropriate. But she was holding on to this.

It was time to leave. An inner voice said: "Pray for her." I didn't want to. It was already tough going and I had come to the point of feeling that there was nothing else I could possibly do for her.

"Pray for her."

So once again I asked her if she'd like me to pray. Once again she nodded and I was also surprised to hear the gratitude in her voice. But yet again prayer was a battle with unseen forces, like going uphill in weighted boots – heavy, difficult, a battle to get the words out. The opposition certainly objected to prayer every time. Looking back I now realise he knew more about the power of prayer than I did at that time, and it scared him. Hallelujah! I persisted and I felt my stubborn streak rise to the surface as I silently faced the enemy and vowed that if prayer was what he was opposed to then prayer was what he was going to have to listen to!

I left feeling drained and subdued – it had been quite a battle. I went straight to our priest-in-charge and we had a long chat. I poured out my heart and he nodded in agreement. His only query was: Does a Christian who dies as a result of suicide lose their salvation? Both of us were uncomfortable about this and had to leave it with God. I told him that I believed Lyndsey was so bound by the enemy in deep areas of her life that she was incapable of doing anything for herself. She had come to our church but, as a church, we were out of our depth, and we couldn't con ourselves that mentioning her name in the list on a Sunday morning was going to shift the enemy from her life. She needed deliverance and to me this whole situation was exposing all our powerlessness and helplessness. I admitted that at first I really didn't want to know, and he agreed.

And so we talked and we prayed together; we felt a bit shaken – her life was very much at stake. I went home and got on my knees again and prayed again, the only way that God was now teaching me to. I rebuked the enemy in Jesus' Name; I claimed her salvation, and asked the Lord to keep the thread that remained of her life safe, until she had found Him and had been set free.

A couple of months later she moved to the Christian treatment centre in Brentwood. Jennifer spoke to her on the phone there and realised that for the time being we needed to give her some space. She needed to make a break with the past and make a new start, and so we dropped out of her picture over the next nine months or so, committing her into God's safe hands. The next news we got was that Lyndsey was moving with several staff to Sussex, to a place near Robertsbridge. They were going to set up another small Christian counselling centre and Lyndsey was joining them as a patient/helper, eventually to work on the team with them as a member of staff. My heart leapt for joy. That spoke volumes of the changes that must have taken place in her life, and the ongoing healing. I was confident that God would do a complete work and use her to help others. That's what He does with lives available for His calling and service, as I was beginning to learn for myself.

And so back to where I started this chapter – the next contact I had with Lyndsey was a letter received in May 1981. She was 'full of beans' as my mum used to say! The new place was called WAY and was now established and running smoothly. It provided quiet refuge and counselling in a small residential home run by a couple of Christian psychiatrists. It seemed that Lyndsey was living in, still having treatment, but now also working in the office.

What did make me sit up was a brief reference to her having recently had a "spiritual awakening," and "feeling all happy inside." For Lyndsey to be feeling all happy inside was a miracle in itself, but what did it all mean, I wonder?

The answer to that came in a letter later from Lyndsey in September enclosing a newsletter of WAY. There, in a section concerning residents and ex-patients, I read: "*Lyndsey* is still at Green Hedges, although fully recovered. *She became a Christian* whilst here and is now serving others through becoming a uniformed member of the St John's Ambulance Association."

So that was it! She'd finally been converted and found the Lord; she'd clearly passed from darkness to light. Graphic past memories flooded my mind. On reading her letter accompanying the newsletter this was really confirmed. It was full of light and joy and love bubbling over. She was obviously amazed at how much she had changed in six months. To quote her:

'Someone said to me once – "Lyndsey, steel is the strongest metal there is, but it has to go through the furnace first!"

'That is very true,' she wrote, 'the Lord has made me stronger than I ever thought possible!'

As my mind flashed back to the part of her life I'd witnessed, I felt such a surge of gratitude to God for His Love and His Grace, and how He met Lyndsey in the darkest darkness, and brought her out into His Glorious Light!

A few weeks later she came to visit and spent several hours with us. All that she had written was confirmed in her face the moment I opened the door to her, and she opened her arms to give me the biggest of hugs, whispering "thank you, thank you" over and over in my ear. My heart was full and all I could say was: "Thank you, thank you, Jesus."

Chapter 15

CARMEN AND THE STRONGMAN

*Whatever you bind on earth will be bound in
Heaven...Matthew 16:19*

THE YEARS WENT BY and God continued to teach and train me and others, on how to be good soldiers in the army whose leader is the Captain of the Lord of Hosts...Jesus Christ Himself. There had been a number of scary lessons, but each one was building, by experience, on the teaching of the Word of God. I loved the Scriptures; I couldn't get enough of them; I was always hungry for more. And I knew that this was the work of the Holy Spirit living in me. My flesh may have been a wee bit curious over previous years but I never had any real desire for the Word like I did now.

And that is all God desires – those who are continually exposing themselves to His Word and His Spirit are those who are continually available to Him. And I was quick to learn that with God there are no coincidences...just His *incidences!* I was constantly being taken by surprise. Sometimes, sad to say, I chickened out, usually out of fear. But I was determined eventually to eliminate those occasions; I wanted always to be ready to respond to the call:

"Go, I am sending you!"

As I said in the last chapter, I have picked out two very different learning situations from the Lord. With Lyndsey it was more of a distance run, learning lesson after lesson for the first time as I chose to keep going. The God-ordained encounter with Carmen was no more that ten to fifteen minutes in total. But apart from that the situation was very similar with God's results bringing glory to Him and freedom to a much-damaged person.

It was 1989, nearly nine years after my first meeting with Lyndsey. I had been on the chaplaincy team at the local hospital for about eighteen months, definitely a call from God, confirmed by my own minister and then the Anglican priest leading the work. It was rarely mundane…often full of surprises, with my spiritual education continuing! Carmen was one of those surprises.

I'd been away on holiday and I wasn't expected in until the following Tuesday. This was the Friday before; I had some free time and I felt drawn, in that almost intangible way that I had begun to recognise, to go up to the hospital – just a short visit perhaps, maybe half-an-hour, to see who was on the ward…any old friends back in for treatment…anyone the Lord may lead me to visit!

I followed my usual routine of going to the office to sign in, leave my coat and pick up a Gideon's Bible. Then I went into the chapel for a few minutes' prayer before going onto the ward I was assigned to. I went into the chapel from the front end by the vestry door. I'd always found the chapel empty at these times and was surprised to see a woman sitting in the far end of the front row. She immediately looked up at the sound of the door opening and she looked a little taken aback. Momentarily

I thought – 'I'll leave her in peace. And I won't feel free to pray either.'

As I'm usually alone I tend to pray aloud. But I felt restrained by the Holy Spirit and led to sit where I usually sit – in the row behind the woman, at the opposite end of the row. As I sat she looked up again, turned around and stared at me for several seconds. At that I realised two things. The first, she was disturbed by my entrance, and secondly, I was very disturbed at the look she gave me. My heart started to beat quickly and I felt tense.

'What on earth is this?' I silently asked the Lord.

I immediately got some sort of understanding that I was up against something demonic.

'Surely not,' I thought, taking in afresh that the woman was in the chapel and reading a gospel from the bookrack.

I sat down and decided to get on with what I'd come into the chapel for. I took the Gideon Bible and opened it. I became aware that the woman was again turning around and looking at me. I realised she was trying to read my name label. I offered her the information that I was a Chaplaincy Assistant and usually came into the chapel for a few minutes to pray before visiting my ward. I asked her if I was disturbing her, and she replied that she had come in for some peace and quiet but… "No, I suppose it is all right." She returned to her reading and I to my praying.

No more than a minute passed and she spoke again. Whether I was listening or not (*and I was*), she started to share her problems. She indeed was an angry woman who didn't want to be in hospital and felt everyone – her husband, family, and all hospital staff – were all ganging up on her. I'm not medically qualified to make a diagnosis but I silently made a private one as I listened to the intermittent tirade from her lips.

She sounded paranoid and I guessed she was a patient from the psychiatric ward. From what she was saying she was in hospital against her will...her husband had had her put here – he was trying to get rid of her and steal the baby.

I was beginning to feel sorry for her husband as I glimpsed a little of what he was having to cope with. I was beginning to feel very worn and frayed myself after only ten minutes with her, but compassion began to rise in my heart for her. When there was a lull I asked her specific but non-threatening questions to indicate that I was interested in what she had to say, and also that I was neutral...not one of those ganging up on her. She responded, sharing more and more of herself and how she was feeling. It was strange – she would start talking quietly and reasonably, but it would build into a crescendo – a loud and threatening tirade of accusations, and anger, and threats to 'get them back' and get her lawyer on to them.

I'm sure the psychiatrist was familiar with this pattern of behaviour, but it was new to me. I'm sure he'd have a name for it, but I was seeing something different in this woman – the demonic. I certainly wouldn't use the word 'possession' here, but I had no doubt that I was in the company of someone demonised – controlled to some degree by unclean spirits. The effect on me was enough to be sure of that. There was without doubt a confrontation going on, between the Holy Spirit in me and the demons in her. The demons didn't like me – that's for sure – and I was in a battle.

I decided to be a little more direct to see what would be exposed. I asked her if she was able to talk to her friends.

"I have no friends!" she flashed back.

I pursued evenly, "It is times of trouble like this that you discover who your real friends are. Acquaintances disappear but you are usually left with one or two people who will stick by you."

Her eyes darkened again and anger began to burn in them.

"I've told you I have no friends," she said. "They've all left me…all turned against me. My husband has seen to that. They are all wrong…all have ganged up against me…"

I pushed further: "If what you are saying you really believe to be true, then I think we may have pinpointed a big part of your problem to be you, yourself. Let's start with *you* and see if we can find out why everyone seems to have given up on you."

With that she erupted. She jumped to her feet and raised her voice menacingly at me, shouting:

"I came in here for peace and quiet, and you are disturbing me. I don't have to take this…everyone is against me…they are all wrong…I'm leaving…"

The tirade continued as she came past me, stopping momentarily beside me far too close for my comfort. She was looking at me intensely and shouting. I knew what I had stirred up, and I instinctively knew I had to look at her, holding steady eye contact with her until she had moved away and had gone out of the door, talking all the way. As she moved away I instantly knew that if I hadn't looked her steadily in the eye as she walked past me, then she would have hit me!

I sat for a moment feeling as though I'd been dragged through a hedge backwards. I was shaking and trembling, my heart was thumping and I had a throbbing headache. I had had a run-in with the demonic and I was feeling the worse for wear, and also felt so sorry for this young woman.

Anger began to rise up in me. "I'm not putting up with that," I voiced.

So I started to pray and I began to come against the powers of darkness that were still pressing in upon me in that chapel. But as I prayed the headache worsened. It was totally distracting – I went to get up and go on the ward, but I was stopped in my tracks by a clear word from the Lord:

"Stay put, I'm sending her back to you."

"What, Lord!?" But I'd heard all right, and I'd heard clearly. "If you are sending her back in, Lord, then there is something You want to do. I must be prepared this time. Show me how, Lord."

The words then came to mind – "Bind the strongman…" For weeks now the Lord had been speaking of and teaching us concerning these things in Scripture. His words to us had been: "Bind the strongman and rob him of his goods and set the captives free."

This was secret closet prayer strategy. He'd already showed us what was required in relation to the Billy Graham Live-link. What a lot of effort, man-hours, time, money, prayer, was going into this. *But* if the strongman over Ashford isn't bound the results will be minimal. The Gospel will go out, and there are people who need to hear it, maybe really want to hear, but unless the spirit that binds them are themselves bound, then these people will not be free to receive or respond to the Good News. We were beginning to learn that this side of intercession was vital in God's strategy for extending is Kingdom.

And now the Lord was saying to me: "Sue, bind the strongman…"

So I started to do just that, this time confident of my authority because I'd had a direct word of instruction from my God. I began by declaring aloud who I was in Christ, and the authority I have in Him. I was reminding myself and building up my own faith, but also reminding the enemy who I was – a child of the Living God, a co-heir with Christ, with Christ's authority over the enemy. I declared to the unclean spirits whom I sensed were already backtracking a bit:

"*YOU* know who I am in Christ; I know who I am in Christ. And you know that I know! You can't bluff through this one. So get out in Jesus' Name."

I moved into spiritual warfare specifically, taking authority over the demons that had been harassing me, and then binding, in Jesus' Name, the demons that held Carmen in bondage. I meant business; I was not playing games and I sensed in my spirit that the enemy knew it too. I had *real* authority – he had *none*, and I was confident of the Lord's continued leading. He had countersigned all that I'd just proclaimed. I was relaxing, the headache was lessening, and the sense of God's presence was lovely.

I picked up my Gideon Bible and opened it at Page 26. As I started to read I heard the door open behind me. Carmen walked back in and came close by me. *But* I had peace this time…real Peace.

She spoke – "I won't be questioned and harassed. I've come to sit quiet and I don't want my peace disturbed." I smiled to myself, listening to the words she was using! She was not shouting – in fact, I sensed a bit of embarrassment at coming back in, and she felt she had to say something.

I smiled again: 'Lord, I don't think she yet realises that You have brought her back in here!' I silently prayed.

She sat down again in the row in front of me. I spoke quietly to her: "I am sorry if I disturbed your peace."

Then I let the whole thing go, turned to my Gideon Bible and started to read.

I read: "*If any of you lack wisdom he should ask God who gives generously.*" I silently prayed – 'Lord, give me wisdom.'

I continued to read: "*Be self-controlled and alert; your enemy, the devil, prowls around like a roaring lion looking for someone to devour. Resist him, standing firm in the faith.*"1 Peter 5:8.

Silently, I spoke – 'Satan, I resist you and stand firm in the faith of Jesus Christ. I take authority over you in Jesus' Name. You have no authority here.'

I continued to read the Scriptures and pray, continually praying in the Spirit as I did so.

Suddenly Carmen spoke: "This is what I mean. This is what is happening to me."

I went over to her. She had found in the Bible the passage concerning Jesus before the council of elders, where He is accused by them. Starting with that very Scripture, because God had given it to her, He gave the application of that word for her life. I was able to share with her *Jesus the Saviour*, who rescues us from a life of darkness, strife, and sin, and who changes our lives as we trust Him. I shared my personal testimony of how my own life had been changed by Jesus.

She became quieter…the restless turmoil subsided as she listened. She also became alert and interested and eager to know more, asking many questions and honestly sharing her own basic beliefs. I was able to relate something of her experience to my own testimony, and present Jesus as the only answer for my life…and for hers.

There was a moment when enough was said, and I knew it. She slowly rose, very thoughtful, saying she was feeling so much better. She admitted she had come in to pray 'Help!' as she could see no way out; and now she was beginning to realise her prayer was being answered. She left quietly, in a peaceful frame of mind, and with her eyes shining this time. That's what made the greatest impact on me…her eyes! The eyes are truly the windows of the soul. The first time she had walked out her eyes were dark, dull, and threatening, and my heart had known I was up against the demonic. This time she left with light in her eyes…fairly sparkling. I was excited as I realised the significance of what had been going on. Maybe at some time in the future she could need some deliverance ministry, but for this particular moment God had done something wonderful. Of that I was convinced.

For myself I was yet again a raw recruit in training in the Lord's army. He had shown me the effects of binding the strongman that the captive may be free. And she was! He showed me how to pray effectively and bind demons whilst praying in the secret place…just me and Him! And it worked! For the second conversation was totally different to the first. In the first she was in demonic bondage and could only express things from the enemy – anger, hatred, resentment… Because the enemy was not bound I was on the receiving end of this bombardment and extremely harassed.

The second conversation came after the Lord had shown me how to take authority. Carmen was now free enough to listen to the Word of God, hear the Gospel, and receive from Jesus. I was also able to share with her what the Lord was giving me to share. I realised that demons were still present but bound and immobilised. All they could do was watch and listen as Carmen and I looked at Scripture together and I was able to share Jesus with her without interference. The strongman was bound and was now a spectator. Praise God. What Love…what Grace! There is so much more to be learned in the strategy of spiritual warfare. 'Oh that I would have a teachable spirit, Lord.'

Postscript.

At the Chaplaincy meeting that evening the Chaplain came up to me with a beaming smile on his face. Was it me who had spent time with a woman from the psychiatric ward this morning? Momentarily I hoped I wasn't in trouble. He had visited Carmen on the ward earlier that day, and found a woman transformed. Expecting the usual difficult time with her, he was amazed. And as she eagerly related how much better she was and why, he realised God had done a very special work that day in that lady's life.

"If she wasn't a Christian before, she certainly is now," he remarked. And the staff were so pleased with the change in her condition they were planning to discharge her the next day.

Apparently the phrase she kept repeating was... 'such peace, such peace...it's wonderful.' Such a sense of peace in my experience is simply the immediate and real presence of Jesus, who is the Prince of Peace. I've lost count of the number of times when Peace has swept over me in the midst of deep trouble, and I know I am surrounded by the intimate presence of Jesus. How I love Him...

Chapter 16

MUM, YOU NEVER DID THAT

And He took the children in His arms, put His
hands on them and blessed them. Mark 10:16

IN JUNE 1991 a small group of us went off to Brighton to the first Ellel Ministries Conference called *The Battle Belongs to the Lord*. What marvellous confirmation there was there, that all we had been learning over five difficult years back in Ashford was the teaching of the Holy Spirit. We saw mature application of things God had been teaching us concerning the ministry of healing and deliverance. We came back with tremendous confidence that we were in the right place with God as He developed (and continues to develop) this area of Jesus' ministry in our fellowship.

There was very much a personal application, too, and it was a very blessed time as I sat under a distinct anointing of the Holy Spirit the whole time. God knew what He was doing; I had no idea. But there were stirrings going on within me as He put His finger on things in my life that He was dealing with and was going to continue with in such areas as emotional healing and deliverance from all the power of the enemy.

God had His agenda and His timing, as I had already discovered over the years. How much I would have preferred to deal with all problems with one prayer. He had shown me six months before that if the roots are not dealt with, then they can grow new branches, and the deep healing He was intending for me would involve Him reaching down to roots that were so deep only He could reach them. I had consented, with trembling, and I sensed that He was on the move with me this week in Brighton.

On the Thursday afternoon we walked over to the Brighton Pavilion for a workshop with Peter Horrobin on *Preparing a Person to Receive Healing and Deliverance*. There was teaching for people who had been rejected in childhood – unwanted pregnancies, unloved children, those whose parents had wanted a boy instead of a girl and vice versa. Powerful ministry took place as a lot of hurts from so far back came to the surface and God healed people and set them free. It was wonderful to watch, and really that's all I was at first – a spectator. For the Holy Spirit led me into a time of worship whilst all this was going on, and I was singing in the Spirit in a way I hadn't experienced before. I was in the intimate presence of God and time stopped still. And I just kept singing! It was as though my praise was ebbing and flowing under the Spirit's momentum.

Gradually I became aware of something stirring deep within me that at first felt like sadness. But as it grew I could feel my body reacting to it. It was like convulsions of sadness going round and round inside of me with no release. I wanted to cry out but I couldn't. Muscles all over my body started to twitch spasmodically, and still no release came. The tension was causing my body to ache. Thelma asked me if I was okay. I had no answer; I couldn't explain. But the spasms and twitching and engulfing feelings of sadness continued. There was no outlet. Thelma and Garry happened to be sitting either side of me and they put their arms around me and quietly prayed.

Gradually it subsided. I felt at peace but very subdued. None of us had a clue what was going on or how to deal with it, or what triggered it in the first place. As we left the meeting Thelma said to me: "Your emotions are bound."

She may be right, I thought. And I quietly put it into God's hands. I was soon to discover that He was already at work and was going to continue what He had started…

It was the next evening at the conference and we were all gathered in the main auditorium. Peter Horrobin was teaching on *How to minister Healing*. I was very interested from a ministering angle. We needed good teaching on this. But as he started to speak specifically about emotional healing I felt again that stirring inside of me.

He continued to speak concerning:

- Blocked, damaged and repressed emotions.
- The different ways that damage happens.
- The many results of emotional damage.

I knew he was speaking directly to me. I knew that God was using this man's mouth to speak directly to me, and it was as though I was the only person in the room.

He stopped his teaching and said the Holy Spirit was already putting the finger of God on some very painful areas in people's lives, *and* what God was touching *He would heal*. He asked those to stand to whom God was speaking. *I stood*…no hesitation. I stood. That action alone I knew was a breakthrough. I was acknowledging perhaps for the first time in front of others, that I had problems in this area of the emotions. In that moment the fear of rejection became weaker than the desire to be healed. And you know – that's all God wants – *our willingness. He will do the rest.*

As I stood I desperately wanted to cry…and I couldn't…I'd been here before. I'd never been able to cry in front of anyone.

A counsellor came and stood quietly beside me. I froze. I couldn't carry on with God with her standing there. Bless her for her sensitivity; after a minute or so she stepped back, leaving me alone with God. I started to talk to Him about it all – what He was touching, how I felt…really felt, giving Him my deepest needs…asking Him to set me free.

Inside of myself I was sobbing violently and nothing was reaching the surface. It was like water rushing into my chest and building up behind a thick dam wall, and the rising pressure was actually causing physical pain, and I found myself doubling over to try and ease it.

I felt a hand on my shoulder and a woman's voice –

"Is it a problem with your father?"

"No, my mother." The revelation was instantaneous.

"Can you forgive her?"

The question was like a switch…an *off* switch. It was as though I'd died on the spot. For a while I stood motionless…I felt absolutely nothing…no reaction to the question at all. Then in the stillness the Holy Spirit spoke:

'Now is the time for an act of will.'

So I then said quietly: "Yes, I can forgive her." I meant it.

She said: "Say – 'Mum, I forgive you'."

"Mum, I forgive you."

A great sob followed the words out and then…NOTHING. It was as though a door had opened and then closed very quickly.

The words came to mind, 'Nothing is too difficult for Thee.'

I whispered, "Lord, could this one be too difficult?"

Again I felt the counsellor draw away, leaving me alone with the Lord. I was beginning to really appreciate her sensitivity.

The Holy Spirit spoke again –

'Just drop onto your knees.' Being at the end of a row the only space was in the aisle. I dropped onto my knees.

He spoke – 'Keep saying it.'

I obeyed.

"Mum, I forgive you…Mum, I forgive you…"

Each time I spoke it, it was as though the dam wall started to crack, and bulge, and break. And the water began to flow. I said it maybe five or six times, and I started to cry…like I've never cried before. I cried loudly, but it didn't matter any more that there were people all around – two and a half thousand in fact, and even more significantly that nearby were people who knew me. It just didn't matter any more. It was just Jesus and me. I had no fear of rejection, just a growing sense of release and healing. At one point as I heard myself crying I thought –

'Sue, you sound like a little child.' And that was just what I was at that moment.

I would have been content and very grateful to go away with what the Lord had just done, but He hadn't finished. There was more, and He was giving me understanding of what He was doing, what He was healing, why…and the root.

Someone dropped on their knees beside me. I didn't look up but I assumed it was the same lady. She put her arm gently around me, and started stroking my hair. *THAT'S ALL…that's all she did*…and yet I cannot really explain the effect that had on me. All sorts of memories flooded back, and as I continued to cry, I was saying over and over –

"Mum, you never did that…you never did that."

I saw vividly times when as a child I'd been upset or naughty, and punished. And never on any occasion could I remember my mum...or anyone coming to comfort me. I'd always cried alone, and I'd ached for someone to put their arms around me, and tell me –

"It's all right."

I gradually learned to take myself off to cry in places where I couldn't be heard and therefore couldn't be rejected and hurt even more. No wonder I'd continued to do the same thing into adulthood, even as a Christian, and even Peter, my husband, never got to know of such times.

And now this woman was being my mum, for just a moment – the mum that the child in me had longed for and ached for, and never knew. And in those few moments, as I sobbed, and this woman stroked my hair like a 'mum', God just poured in His healing.

There was a divine exchange of emotions going on in my soul – the negative ones that had accumulated for over forty years being replaced by healthy positive ones – love for fear, security for insecurity, acceptance for rejection...and much more. God was healing at a depth that only He could touch. I leaned towards my 'temporary' mum and she tucked my head under her chin, and she held my head close and continued to gently stroke my hair.

The Holy Spirit gave me just one final revelation that completed what He was doing at that particular time...the revelation that my mum couldn't help it; her need had been greater than mine; that what she couldn't give to me, she hadn't received herself as a child. *It wasn't her fault; there wasn't any blame.* I understood too that I had carried the *guilt* of this with me. Because even as a child I had recognised something of my mum's need and her deep unhappiness, and I had not been able to meet her need in any way myself.

I spoke once – "I'm sorry, Mum."

The guilt went, the weeping subsided, and the Peace of God settled in my heart. I looked up into the face of the woman who'd been my 'mum' for just a few minutes. And I saw in her face simply – *the compassion of Jesus*, and I knew He'd done it all. I knew too that she'd been willing to be His channel for the moment, and I was greatly challenged by that. God knew I had prayed desperate prayers for so long to be free from all irrational fears and phobias so I could be available for Him to use in His service at any time. He knew my heart, and He meant serious business and was answering my prayers. I sat down, fresh and washed, and clean, and healed...and free some more...

"It is for freedom that He has, and is, setting me free." Hallelujah, oh Gracious Lord!

Chapter 17

AN ORDINARY LADY TOUCHED BY AN EXTRAORDINARY GOD

*For God so loved the world that He gave His one
and only Son, that whosoever believes and trusts
in Him shall not perish but have Eternal Life.
John 3:16*

WHEN MY HEART was invaded by the Love of God in those early days, that was when I began to Love Him, really love Him. I fell in love with Jesus. I found I loved God in return with the same love He loved me. And I began to love others with the love of God. Self-effort had no part in this. God loved me into loving with His Love. I had a love for others like I'd never had before. And I loved to see God touching people with His Love. Sometimes it was from a distance and all I had to do was pray. Other times He drew me in to share His love more personally. I've seen so many people touched by God, and been overwhelmed, overjoyed, and privileged to witness miracles, even in the dying.

Peggy Horn died on the morning of 22nd January 1985, at the age of fifty-five. The cancer that worked quickly through her body in a few months did not get her in the end.
JESUS DID!

I'd known her for about sixteen years since she, Len, and their son had moved into a semi opposite. When our son Ian was born she became our regular babysitter, and she was very fond of him. I saw a lot of her for about three years. Then circumstances changed and we saw less and less of her. We had another baby, Christine. She got a job in Sainsbury's, and her son got a girlfriend, and they married. From 1974 to the end of 1984 we exchanged Christmas cards and chatted if we met in the street.

My heart went out to her husband when I heard he had shingles. I recall the pain that an elderly friend was still enduring in her face and neck five years after contracting shingles, and I felt compassion for this sick man. So I popped in to see if there was anything I could do. No, they had everything covered, but prayer was mentioned rather coyly by Peggy. I had never had the opportunity to witness to her since my conversion, but maybe they had seen us going to church each Sunday morning. So yes, I promised to pray for Len, and when I sought God it felt right to pray for physical healing. I heard that Len made a very speedy recovery. Did they make the connection, I wondered?

It was early October 1984 that I heard that Peggy wasn't feeling well at all. She had put up with nausea and abdominal pain for some time before going to the doctors. Had she gone immediately the outcome could have been very different, but I knew her well enough from the old days that fear would have been the reason...and I knew what that felt like. She finally went to her GP, who sent her to the hospital. The next report I got from her near neighbour was that she was going to Canterbury Hospital for radiotherapy. That spoke to me of one thing – *cancer*. Working in the surgery myself I soon got solid confirmation of that. It was very serious and she was going to

Canterbury by ambulance four days a week. The district nurse explained she was in considerable pain and discomfort, and very, very frightened.

I cried for her – I could almost feel her fear. I started to pray in earnest for her for the first time. Oh, how I knew she needed Jesus. I prayed for an opportunity to talk to her about the Saviour.

One Saturday morning I picked up an elderly neighbour for our regular trip to Sainsbury's, and just popped into Peggy's to see if Len wanted to come with us to do his shopping; neither of them drove. Peggy was standing at the kitchen sink. She couldn't keep still. She was literally hopping from one foot to the other, and writhing in considerable discomfort. She had lost weight. But what shocked me most of all was her voice. It was tiny and weak and full of fear. She sat down and briefly shared how she was feeling and what was going on. Tears came to her eyes; she looked at me and said:

"Sue, when you go to church tomorrow, say a prayer for me."

"Not just Sunday Peggy, but every day I will pray." I quickly bent down, put my arm around her, kissed the top of her head and left, with the promise that I'd come back to talk to her sometime.

"Yes please," she replied.

I went away thinking this was the opening I had been praying about – now I could go in, sit down with her, and tell her about Jesus, the Saviour. Nothing wrong in that, but it didn't happen to be part of God's plan in this situation. So the next couple of visits seemed to be fruitless in this direction. So back to the prayer closet –

"Lord, I'm desperate for her…she's dying…she needs You Jesus more than anything – how? Lord, how?"

His reply was clear – '*You pray*...I'll do the work.'

"All right Lord. I do find it difficult to pray in secret and watch her dying without saying a word. So please tell me what to pray for. Give me a list Lord. I want to know I'm praying your will in this."

And He did! He gave me three things to pray for, which I did alone for two weeks, and then on a Lydia Prayer day I shared with my Lydia prayer partner, and we prayed together those three things and were confident in our hearts of God's answer. It was so good that day to pray through with someone else – the confirmation in our hearts was tremendous. And as usual God's timing was perfect. At the beginning of our prayer day we saw the ambulance arrive to pick Peggy up for her radiotherapy. Several hours later we saw the ambulance return her home. My Lydia prayer partner never met Peggy and that was all she ever saw of her, but we prayed for her with one heart and mind as God led us. I wrote down in my Lydia diary for that day those three things God had led us to pray about –

1) To come against a spirit of fear.
2) To pray the Peace of Jesus into her life.
3) To pray that she may *know* Him.

There was no leading to pray for physical healing as such – tough in the face of such suffering. But we were obedient as far as we understood what God was saying and we left it with Him.

The next month passed quickly – Christmas came and went, and we saw the New Year in. I only saw Peggy a few times as we ourselves were almost totally preoccupied with sorting out the future for Peter's mum. She was no longer safe in her own home, and stayed with us over Christmas and

New Year, whilst we awaited a vacancy in the home chosen for her by her daughters. Talking to Peggy about this caused her to reminisce over the past – early days babysitting for Ian, trips we took her on to mother-in-law's farm in the Alkham valley. It was obviously doing her good to talk; the good memories were an encouragement to both of us, and drew me closer to her once again.

The January 8 dawned – another snowy and bitterly cold day. I came downstairs early for my quiet time and saw the doctor's car outside Peggy's. Then the ambulance arrived. I found out she had been admitted with mysterious pains in her side and more tests were to follow. Two days later after dropping Peter off at work I went straight to the hospital to see her. The first person I met was Raz, or Sister Ramiah, to give her proper title. It was so good to meet such a lovely sister in Jesus and friend from church.

Peggy looked ever so pleased to see me. I grabbed a chair from the corridor and sat down by her bed. She obviously was eager to talk and with preliminary greetings over there was no stopping her, not that I wanted to interrupt what I was hearing. I just listened, mouth open in astonishment most of the time!

She had turned to prayer…and it worked! She had started to pray out of desperation early in her illness, a few months back – she was in so much pain, and fear. She couldn't put a date to it but something happened to her that she found difficult to explain or understand. And she'd bottled it all up, speaking to no one. She was bursting to talk to someone, and when I walked into the ward she decided that someone was me. I felt so privileged to listen to her, and so grateful to the Lord for the time we shared together that day.

Peggy was not a churchgoer, not a religious person in any way, and had no theological language to explain with. How refreshing that was. For what she shared was not only simple and natural, but came from a depth of an experience with God in the midst of suffering, that was too deep for me to understand fully, but knowing Jesus in my own heart I just witnessed to the authenticity of all she was saying. I was able to agree with her, show understanding, and encourage her. That seemed to open her up even more as she felt the freedom to continue to share such very precious and personal things.

Where was the Peggy I had known who was very private, keeping her distance, and never talking about the deeper things in life? She was gone! This was a new Peggy in her place, pouring out her heart. What a miracle God was doing with this woman.

I encouraged her to share more – what had been, and what was happening in her life as a result of the initial decision to pray.

Well, first she found that very specific prayers were being answered – prayers concerned with different pains that she couldn't cope with, swollen legs, catheters, sleepless nights…all sorts of very practical things she was desperate about. To her delight, and at first great surprise, the answers were very clear.

Then there was the paralysing fear she had from early on in her illness. How awful it was; how she wouldn't let Len out of her sight, and needed someone with her every moment because she was so frightened.

"Has that fear gone now, Peggy?" I asked.

"Oh yes," she smiled, "and now I have a peace…even now I have a tremendous peace that I can't explain."

My mind raced back over the three things God had given me to pray. 'Golly,' I thought, 'she's already confirmed the first two – the spirit of fear has been broken, praise God!' Then, although as yet she hadn't mentioned Jesus, she was most definitely describing His wonderful Peace in her heart.

Those two were now confirming the third – that she may know Him. Undoubtedly God was making Himself known to her in a beautiful and deep way. He was doing it *His way.* And so I said to her –

"God has become very real to you Peggy, hasn't He?"

"Oh yes," she replied. "He's so close it's as though He's holding my hand."

"Peggy, all that you have said and all that I know, I put one word to describe it for you – *JESUS* – it is Jesus Himself Who has drawn close to you, made Himself know to you...made God real. Jesus *IS* the way to the Father. He really is the Saviour."

"Yes He is," she replied, "He's the only Saviour I've got...and I need Him so much."

She was there before me! Every time she opened her mouth it fairly took my breath away to hear what she had to say. She was on a roll with the Holy Spirit! As I listened and shared with her I was in a continual state of Joy, mixed with overwhelming gratitude to the Lord. My heart kept saying – "Thank You, thank You" – and that was inadequate to describe how I was feeling, but He knew.

I told Peggy that I knew Raz and she loved Jesus too. She asked me to call Raz over, which I did, and Peggy continued to share with her. She was dying apparently, but she had vitality that I'd never seen in Peggy before...physical weakness, but spiritual strength.

I was sure she must be tiring with all this excitement, but every attempt I made to leave was thwarted with her having something else to say. She explained how she had needed to release all she had stored up over the past weeks. She finally reached out and took both my hands, held them tightly and said –

"Will you pray with me before you go, Sue?"

I was choked…but delighted. "Yes," I whispered. And so we prayed, holding tightly on to one another, but most of all holding tightly onto the Lord. And His Peace…His Presence, surrounded us, in one of those supernatural moments that you don't want ever to lose and time seems to stand still.

I stood up to go, but found I just didn't want to move. And so I stood silently by her bed for several minutes. Neither of us said a word. The prayer hadn't finished with the 'Amen'. It continued in the silence, because He was still communing with us. The fragrance of Jesus is so sweet…so precious. I wondered if Peggy was feeling as I was in that moment. I looked toward her. Her eyes didn't meet mine. Yes, they were open, but she was looking right past me, and looked so content and peaceful. I looked toward the doorway of the bay where she seemed to be looking, but I saw nobody.

Still looking she spoke – "Dear, dear Jesus," she said and my heart leapt inside me. Now I guessed who she could see, and who I couldn't!

"Dear Jesus…how wonderful He is!"

I looked at her intently and said – "Peggy, it sounds as though you love Him."

"Oh yes, I love Him…I love Him very, very much." She slowly looked back at me as she spoke.

"I love Him too, Peggy," I smiled. She took my hands again…I kissed her and left.

Twelve days later Peggy died. I saw her several times before then. We talked quietly together; she always wanted to pray, and seemed immensely grateful and comforted with any Scriptures I read to her. She was delighted, too, that my minister "had found time to visit me." He too had talked and prayed with her.

All day on the 21st January I felt very restless. It was Peggy, I was sure. She had come home from hospital on Friday 18th to spend some time with Len. The restlessness I felt built up over the weekend. I wondered how Len was coping but there was also their son and his wife, and I felt the Lord just holding me back from going to the house to see how things were.

By Monday morning I was sure there was a crisis and Peggy was back in hospital. I had seen no comings and going and yet I felt gut sure. How could I find out? I didn't want to ring Len to ask him. I continued to pray for guidance. Mid-morning I rang the hospital and asked whether Mrs Peggy Horn had been re-admitted. Yes, she had. My request to visit was gently turned down – "I'm sorry, next of kin only." I suddenly felt very isolated and lonely. I realised how very close Peggy and I had drawn together in a matter of days. And the nurse's words confirmed what I had begun to suspect – Peggy was close to death. I desperately wanted to see her one more time…to touch her…to spend time with her…to speak with her…just to spend a precious moment with her. I was already grieving – I wouldn't see her again; it's only next of kin…it's only a matter of time.

In prayer I handed it all over to the Lord – a mixture of grief and joy. There was grief at the loss I was feeling, and joy at the knowledge that the cancer had lost. She belonged to Jesus and the cancer was now the servant – hastening her total experience of His presence in Glory. I could see no way of seeing her again, but I had learnt enough to know that if I was meant to then the Lord was quite capable of arranging it, and I felt happy leaving it with Him.

It was much later in the day, walking home from work at the surgery, at about 7.15 p.m. As I walked past Peggy's house I noticed the place was in total darkness.

'Len must be with her,' I thought. The Lord's voice to me was distinctly recognisable –

'*Now* go and visit her.'

I ran up our drive. I was expecting a friend at 7.30 p.m. But I told Peter I was going to the hospital. I ran upstairs and rang the hospital.

"I'm a friend of Peggy Horn. Is her husband there?"

"No, he's not at the moment," was the reply.

"Will it be all right to pop in and see her?"

There was a moment's silence and then – "Yes, that will be okay."

I felt excited; I truly believe that in that moment the Lord had overruled. I hoped they wouldn't change their minds by the time I got there. I rang my friend, told her briefly what was going on and promised to pick her up on the way back from the hospital. With that sorted out I was free to jump into the car and make for the hospital.

I approached the nurse's station and enquired of Peggy's whereabouts. They asked when I had last seen her and warned me she had changed, in order that I might absorb some of the shock in advance. The door of the little single room next to the nurse's station was wedged open. I walked in slowly. I could see the figure in the bed with her head turned away from the door. I took my coat off and put my bag down by the door, and walked around to the other side of the bed. Yes, what I saw was a shock. I'd never been with anyone dying before but I knew I was looking death in the face. Her eyes, when she opened them, stared out and already seemed sightless – I wasn't sure she could see me at all. She had lost more weight, her head seemed smaller and her face sort of shrunken, and there was those staring eyes – I looked steadily into them; it seemed the right thing to do.

I wasn't afraid, although I reckon my heart was beating a little faster than normal. Peggy was very still and except for long steady, but noisy breaths, all she moved were those eyes and occasionally her mouth...or was I imagining that?

In the stillness was a tremendous peace, and I knew the presence of Jesus with us. Those two emotions started to well up in me again – sadness and joy; and that deep love for her that I knew was the Lord's Love for her. And I knew He had brought me here to express it to her. I had no idea how 'conscious' she was, how much she could hear, feel or see, but I knew in my heart the desire and the freedom to express the Love of Jesus in those three ways – touch, voice, look. I searched under the bedclothes for her hand, all the time speaking quietly to her, telling her I wanted to hold her hand. How warm it was – funny, I was expecting it to feel cold. The corners of her mouth flickered. I wondered if she was trying to smile or even speak. My other hand I laid gently on her forehead. I sensed Jesus touching her as I did, using my hands.

I started to talk quietly to her. I went over all the things we'd shared together days before – all that she had shared about Jesus, and how God Had made Himself known to her. There seemed to be a wealth of things to share back with her to remind her. Oh how glad I was we'd talked so openly about the Saviour. How natural and lovely and beautiful it seemed to be able to share Him now. As I talked and looked steadily at her I recognised what looked like an attempted smile on several occasions, and I know we were both appreciating this short time of intimate fellowship with Jesus. How close He felt, how real, and I was certain this was her experience too.

I wondered about the smile at the mention of Jesus' Name. Was I imagining it? Was it wishful thinking on my part? I can remember the early days as a mum when my newborn 'smiled' but everyone else said he had wind!

'Lord, how do I know she can hear me?' The immediate thought came back –

'Ask her if she'd like to pray' –

"Peggy, we're going to pray." No mistaking it – *that* was a smile!

"Would you like me to pray, Peggy?" There it was again, and her lips were moving too as if she were trying to speak.

"Yes, I know Peggy, I know; let's talk to Jesus."

Oh, how good it was to pray with her. How good it felt to know that Jesus was in control. I looked at her and silently prayed –

"Cancer, you *ARE* beaten. Jesus has her. You have done your worst and ended up driving her into His hands. She's found Him, and you are beaten. *Praise God!"*

And that was just how I felt. In that moment I experienced the victory of the Cross. As I looked at Peggy and saw her in the loving arms of her Saviour, death, however inevitable, had lost a lot of its sting for me in that moment. I was so grateful.

I knew it was time to go. A part of me wanted to stay with her, holding her hand until she died. But the Lord was firm – I must go now. I held her for a moment and kissed her. I told her I loved her, that I was going home now, but that He'd never leave her…that I would see her again. I told her the Truth.

I had a phone call after breakfast the next morning. Peggy had died earlier in the morning. I was relieved. Her suffering was over; I was sad, very sad…for Len and David; sad for myself.

But I was overjoyed that she was with Jesus.

Chapter 18

BILL'S MIRACLE

*And if the Spirit of Him who raised Jesus from the
dead is living in you, He who raised Christ from
the dead will also give life to your mortal body
through the Spirit who lives in you. Romans 8:11*

BILL WAS JUST ANOTHER ORDINARY PERSON, a
gentle man who lived a simple life but a life that honoured
the God he trusted, and one day his life was touched by that
same extraordinary God. An elderly gentleman, he was married
to Hannah. They lived in a small council bungalow for the
elderly, and Bill loved his little garden, producing more fruit
and vegetables there than someone with an allotment several
times the size. He even managed to fit a small shed in his tiny
plot and immensely enjoyed pottering away in there at his
woodwork. And he always loved to give away the fruit of his
labour. Bill was a brother in Christ and we worshipped at the
same church.

It was Easter 1995 and a few days earlier Bill had a massive
stroke in his garden and was rushed to the local hospital. On
the grapevine we heard it was touch-and-go for Bill. I woke up
Good Friday morning planning to go to celebrate communion
'at the Cross' as I had done for a number of years. But I felt
restless on rising, and I had a quiet time and as I prayed it
became clear that the Holy Spirit was giving me a nudge to go

and visit Bill, and peace settled in my heart as I decided to do just that. His family would be there in the afternoon, and it's much quieter in the hospital in the morning. Bill had been in the William Harvey Hospital for three days and the stroke had left him paralysed down the left-hand side of his body. The doctors were very concerned because they couldn't stabilise him. They had to keep sedating him heavily because every time he came around he 'fitted'. It appeared that his life was hanging in the balance.

I came onto Bill's ward in my official capacity as a member of the Hospital Chaplain's team, wearing my badge, which clears the way for me to visit patients at any time. Bill appeared to be asleep. He was lying absolutely flat on his back with no pillow. Nevertheless I went and stood beside his bed and watched him quietly for a minute or so before saying –

"Hello, Bill."

I was amazed by the immediate 'hello' back! I'd thought he was deeply asleep, but he wasn't. He didn't open his eyes, but he started to talk to me.

"Do you know who this is, Bill?" I asked.

"Yes, it's Sue," he replied promptly. He still hadn't opened his eyes!

He continued to talk…though a little slurred. I knew he was sedated, but I was so relieved his speech was recovering. I had been given to think otherwise.

Bill kept touching his chest and saying he had indigestion – he seemed to think that lying flat had trapped wind, and he couldn't shift it, and it was causing him quite some pain. I told him I would find a nurse for him. I'd been with him just a few minutes, and thought, 'Well, that was a short visit!'

When I found the nurse and told her of Bill's problem, she looked surprised and said, "Has he been talking to you?"

"Yes," I said.

"That's amazing," she said. "We've been quite concerned. We haven't been able to get more than a grunt out of him for more than twenty-four hours."

I went back to say goodbye to Bill, closely followed by two nurses. They started to pull the curtain around his bed, so I said, "I'll come back again."

"Oh no," said the nurse in charge. "I'd like you to wait…we won't be long…you're obviously doing him some good!"

I knew I hadn't done anything, but I reckoned that God was at work, and maybe He wanted me to stay too! So I sat down again beside Bill. He was obviously much more comfortable. The indigestion had gone, and he was propped up in bed with several pillows.

"Do you know what day it is, Bill?"

"Thursday…or is it Friday?" he asked.

"It's Good Friday, Bill, and all our lot at Willesborough are in church at this moment having their Good Friday morning service." Bill was a regular worshipper and would have been there if he could.

"Heh, so that no one can say sorry we missed it, shall we do our own Good Friday bit here, Bill?"

"Oh yes, that would be good."

I noticed Bill had his Bible on the top of his bedside cabinet, so I asked him if we could use it. I opened it at Mark 15 and read aloud part of the passage of Jesus' death – verses 33-39. We were just thinking on how amazing it was for a Roman centurion to see something in that ghastly event that made him sure that Jesus was the Son of God, when I got a prompting from the Holy Spirit –

'TELL BILL THAT GOOD FRIDAY IS ONLY TEMPORARY.'

"You know Bill, Good Friday is only temporary," I started. "The death of Jesus was only temporary. In three days we have Easter Day, and we celebrate the RESURRECTION. Bill, Resurrection Life is permanent; death is temporary."

I was getting excited as I began to see where God was leading…

Bill opened his eyes briefly and looked straight at me –

"Yes…YES…that's right."

And as I looked at him I knew the Spirit of God was beginning to stir something in his heart. I saw it in him, and I felt it in me. We were under an anointing.

I continued – "Bill, all that has happened to you with this stroke, and the condition you are in now – this is temporary. Bill, this is Good Friday, and Good Friday is temporary, remember. The amazing thing, Bill, is that you and I already know what that centurion didn't know – that Resurrection Day follows Good Friday…and that Resurrection Life is PERMANENT. Bill! You've already got Resurrection Life because you belong to Jesus – and *that's* permanent. What you are going through here, Bill, in your body, is temporary – it won't last! It's to do with Good Friday. But you've already got Life, Bill, real Life – and you've got it permanently. *BILL – HAVE YOU GOT THAT? HAVE YOU GOT IT, BILL?*"

I was really excited by now, because I sensed God was doing something really special.

Bill started to chuckle…and he chuckled, and chuckled. He looked at me and said:

"YES, I'VE GOT IT…I'VE GOT IT!" And he continued to chuckle. For a moment, just a moment, I had an anxious thought –

'What if he doesn't stop laughing and he pegs out? Then I'll get the blame!'

But he did stop, and he lay there quietly with a smile across his face. I looked at him and I knew God had done something. So I said:

"Bill, I'll just pray before I leave."

"Yes please," he replied.

I took his hand. I prayed, briefly, what we had just shared, and I prayed for the Peace of God to rest upon him. It was a matter of seconds, but when I looked up he was asleep, a hint of a smile still on his face. I slipped my hand out of his and quietly left.

I popped in to see Bill a few days later whilst on my regular ward round. He was sitting up, fully conscious, and trying to adjust his pillow behind his head with his 'paralysed' hand!

Not many days later, Bill's wife rang to say that Bill was home. In answer to my enquiry she said they were managing very well. Bill was walking unaided...no Zimmer frame, not even a walking stick!

Medically it shouldn't be this way, so said the doctors involved on his case. The doctor who discharged him wrote in his notes – 'Healed through prayer by God.' He said there was no other way Bill could have recovered like he had done. It was a miracle. Bill was in church the next Sunday giving public testimony to God's healing power. He spoke of his stroke and recovery as an Easter experience – death followed by Resurrection Life.

Praise God that when He gives Life He gives it in abundance, and Bill knew that he had Resurrection life, and that's permanent. Amen.

Chapter 19

BUDDHA, AN ARCHBISHOP, AND JESUS!

Salvation is found in no one else, for there is no other name under heaven given to men by which we must be saved. Acts 4:12

I FIRST MET DIANE in the summer of 1978. I had been a Christian less than a year and I had joined the church's door-to-door team. It was a change to be knocking on doors for Jesus instead of the Liberal Party! One evening I was paired with the vicar and we were out in my own road. We knocked next door but one to my own house. The house had recently been sold but we hadn't yet seen anyone move in…the previous inhabitants had left the blinds on the windows, so you couldn't look in! So I was surprised to see a light on. The door was opened by a slightly built elderly lady. She invited us in when we introduced ourselves, and introduced herself as Diane.

She'd moved in that day but her furniture had not yet caught her up so there were just garden chairs she had borrowed from her nephew in Kennington. She certainly enjoyed talking to us and was pleased to meet a near neighbour. Her story was really interesting. She had married just before war broke out in 1939, and her husband was a teacher in the local boys Grammar school in Ashford, just around the corner, and they bought a three-storey house opposite the entrance to our estate. In those days it was farmland with a large apple orchard. He enlisted with the air force, trained as a gunner, and was tragically killed in a fighter plane eighteen months after their wedding.

Diane, a qualified nurse, decided on a fresh start. She moved to Canada and took up a career in nursing. She never married again and after she retired a few years previously she felt a real longing for the 'homeland'. And with the help of a nephew in Ashford a house was purchased two doors from Peter and me. And the vicar and I were the first locals she met and she seemed delighted.

Her furniture duly arrived later that week and I kept a regular check on her as she settled in. She was a fiercely independent woman, her nephew was very attentive and did things that she couldn't do, and I started taking her to Sainsbury's with me for the weekly shop. One day on returning from such a trip she turned and looked at me as I finished unloading her groceries and said:

"Sue, you always seem so happy and contented. You've always got a sunny smile on your face. What is it about you? Whatever you've got, I want it!"

I said: "Well Di, I know I'm not always like that; I have my ups and downs, but what makes the biggest difference in my life is that I have a Saviour and His name is Jesus. I know Him, I love Him, and He is as real to me as you are standing here beside me."

"Oh, I'd love a saviour like that," she replied.

"You can," I said.

"I wish I had your faith," she said.

"You can," I replied. "Anyone can, it's not exclusive. It's for anyone who will come to Jesus. You talk to Him, Di. You've just got to ask and receive."

Over the next few weeks we talked about God, and I shared the basics of the Good News of the Gospel with her. And I say 'basics' because I was only a babe in Christ. But though I didn't know much in the way of theology, what I did have was treasure indeed – *I knew Him, I loved Him, I had a relationship with Jesus, my Saviour and Lord, and I was passionate about Him.* She had been attracted to something in me, and all I had was Jesus, and having Him was everything.

And so I shared the basics with her of what it meant to be a *real* Christian, and what she needed to do to know Jesus as *her* Saviour. I was not in a rush because in my personal experience God chose His perfect timing to reveal Himself to me. But she was not just making conversation. She was in earnest. So one evening after doing some Bible study together I asked her if she wanted Jesus in her life. "YES!" she said. So I led her in a prayer of repentance and commitment. I left her with some Scriptures to read. Apparently she had a Bible and was in the habit of reading it in bed at night. So I thought that was a good start.

I called on her next day to see how she was. She looked a bit sad and said she didn't *feel* anything happened the night before…didn't *feel* any different. She was obviously disappointed. I told her not to worry, that it was not a matter of feelings but of faith – the feelings would follow later. FAITH was the key, faith in God, trusting that he'd heard the cry of her heart and the prayer she'd prayed; that He'd answered and come into her life.

Over the days and weeks that followed she continued in doubt because she didn't *feel* anything. I felt a bit like the sower with the seed that had been snatched away before it had even a chance to get a root down. And there was only one person who steals like that – the devil. But how?

We continued to build our friendship. We chatted now and again about spiritual things, discussed things in the Bible and did the occasional study. But there was, I believe, some sort of blockage to the spiritual progress that she herself was eager for. She was still earnest to *feel* sure, and "I can't *make* myself believe, can I?" became another phrase she used regularly. I was beginning to feel a bit weary and worn myself, so I did less talking about these things and more praying – what are the blockages, Lord, in her life?

He showed me several things. The first was that she was a fiercely independent old lady, in control of her own life, running it the way she chose and no one else was going to tell her how to. This was as a result of losing her husband at such an early age and never marrying again. In effect she wanted Jesus on her terms, not His. But it doesn't work that way. He requires *surrender* – a real surrendering of our lives to Him, letting Him be not only Saviour but also Lord. Her response: "But I can't *make* myself."

I also had discovered in our chats that she had no problem in seeing Jesus as a man, but great difficulty in seeing Him as God – God who had become man. Warning bells rang here. I'd had a number of encounters with JW's[2] since becoming a Christian, and the Lord was putting His finger on this. So I asked her if she'd had any dealings with JW's. Yes, she'd had them in her home at one time in Canada for a series of Bible studies. So that was the source of her difficulty in believing Jesus is God. She needed to renounce their false teaching and let Him reveal Himself to her as He truly was. I talked this over with her, but she repeated again: "I can't make myself believe." She certainly wasn't ready to deal with that, but the resources of

---

[2] Jehovah's Witnesses.

God were available to me through prayer and I began to use them more and more on her behalf.

Buddha was the next thing God opened my eyes to. She was an avid collector of books and ornaments. On the table beside the door as you walked into the living room was a large figure of Buddha in the traditional lotus position. I had noticed it from the start but thought no more of it until I asked the Lord what were the blockages in her life, and it was as if He pointed to Buddha the next time I walked into her house, and said to me: 'That's a blockage.' I certainly was on a learning curve here, and asked Him for discernment. He showed me that it wasn't just an ornament but an idol, an object of worship. Even though I realised she didn't worship it, she loved it, and had given it pride of place in her home. No wonder she had difficulty feeling the presence of the One True God. He would not share a home with idols, and though she was earnest in her quest she never had assurance of salvation.

I had become very fond of her, and as she got older and more infirm I felt protective of her and sad that spiritually she felt unfulfilled. We had some great times together, though. She was well educated and well read and fascinating to listen to, and this is where the archbishop is to be mentioned. She was proud to be the descendant of Stephen Langton, Archbishop of Canterbury. But of course, just as there is no salvation in Buddha, there is no salvation in being a descendant of an archbishop either! Only Jesus saves, and I prayed He'd get her in the end!

She continued to be a strong willed old lady, running her own life her own way. She argued with the Scriptures that clearly proved Jesus to be exactly who He said He was – both God and man. And as far as Buddha was concerned, he was just a favourite ornament. When she went on holiday she hid him away when I was looking after her house because she didn't want to offend me. I chuckled every time I went in and saw the empty table, and wondered where she had put him! But he appeared back in his pride of place as soon as she arrived home.

She eventually moved away, into a bungalow which was much safer for her, and she was nearer to her nephew who took total responsibility for her care. Apart from Christmas and birthday cards and presents, and the occasional visit, I lost regular contact with Di. I continued to pray, and my enduring prayer for her was:

"Lord, don't let her die until she is firmly in Your Kingdom."

It was in May 1999 that I heard that Di was in the local hospital. I rang Brian her nephew and found out she had cancer of the pancreas and it was inoperable. He said she had only days to live. I wasted no time in going to visit her. That first visit was a bit of a shock. She was very small and frail, had lost weight and was yellow from jaundice. It looked like the liver was in trouble too. She was asleep. She opened her eyes immediately I called her name and we had a real good chinwag. She got the major barrier out of the way quickly. When she told me she was on the way out I was deliberately obtuse and asked her what she meant. I wanted her to do the talking…

She gave me that 'are you thick or what' look and spelt it out: "I'm dying, Sue."

I asked her if she'd got that from the horse's mouth, that is, the doctors. Yes, she had. And did she ask them, or did they tell her? No, she asked them. She wanted no prevaricating on the matter. She insisted on a straight answer, and they gave it to her. I was relieved that she told me this. It cleared out of the way a lot of so-called 'pussy-footing' around the subject. We were in the light with each other. We could talk straight. We both knew, so it wasn't a taboo area we had to avoid.

I've seen too many situations, both in my personal contacts as well as in my hospital chaplaincy work, where the patient has known their prognosis but doesn't want the relatives to know, or the relatives have been told and don't want the patient to know. Just at the time when there is such a need for quality relationship with one another, each is in the dark with the other in a conspiracy of silence.

So Di knew she was dying; I knew she was dying, and she knew that I knew. We had a great natter...no holds barred! She looked very weak but her voice was still strong and she wanted to talk. She seemed remarkably upbeat, above the situation and quite cheerful. There was a serenity I hadn't seen before. She was different. She had always been a talker, but I'd seen that as the consequences of a very intelligent old lady living on her own and needing the stimulation of good conversation. You'd think that being on morphine, but still in pain, stuck in hospital and dying, that she'd be in a bad state of mind. But I'd never known her so positive. I commented on this...how peaceful she seemed. She agreed. I qualified it and asked her if she felt at peace with God. Yes, was her answer.

I went a little further and asked her, what about Jesus? She said I knew she only believed in one God. The JW teaching, that Jehovah alone is God and Jesus is not God the Son, was still lurking. Despite that I was very aware of the presence of God with us, and the Peace of God was touching us both. I felt excited.

"Lord, don't let her die until she knows You," I silently prayed.

I let the subject drop and we started reminiscing about the past. It was great remembering incidences, the laughs we had, the silly things we did...how bossy she was, and how cheeky I was to my elder in return! She cracked up laughing at that. We went hammer and tongs with one another at times, because I was bossy too! We had a hilarious time, laughing and joking, much to the amusement of other patients in the bay.

When I left her, she said: "Come again Sue, please."

Afterwards I had a time of prayer as I walked the dog. I was still fretting concerning her spiritual state. She looked so at peace and she said she was at peace with God…but I still had the theological problem about her struggle to accept Jesus as the Son of God – God come in human flesh. Jesus as merely a man is not the Jesus of the Bible. Again I prayed:

"Don't let her die until she's fully in your Kingdom, Lord."

I was certain of the reality of heaven and hell and that once you've died it's too late to make that decision to surrender one's life to Jesus Christ.

"Lord, where is she in all this? You can see all things. Only You know. But if you want to use me at the eleventh hour I am here, Lord."

I heard a clear response from the Holy Spirit:

"I took her at her word right from the start. I have never let her go and I will finish what I started. Stop fretting, Sue. Your earnest praying will be answered. Let it go, Sue, and leave her to Me. If you fret and fuss about what you should say, then you will not be available to Me to be My mouthpiece when I want you to speak. Lay it all down Sue, wait on Me and just be available to Me."

The second visit was three days later. She was thinner, still very jaundiced and weaker physically. She was asleep but immediately opened her eyes when I spoke her name, and we carried on where we had left off. We joked and laughed and reminisced about the past. She didn't want me to leave – "I love to have someone to talk to," she said. So I stayed until lunchtime when the nurse appeared to raise her from the flat position and to help her with a little food. I gave her a kiss, told her I loved her and said goodbye. She said she loved me and would I please come again. I agreed.

It was a whole week before I visited Di again. I'd picked up some virus that was going around and felt quite rough. I'd wanted to get in to see Di but I knew I couldn't until I was well. When I saw her I got such a shock. In that week she had deteriorated so much. Yes, in those first two visits we both knew she was dying but she certainly did not have that presence, or spirit of death over her. Now she did. I could see it; I could feel it.

She'd shrunk to skin and bone and she seemed to be asleep with her eyes half open. I took her hand from under the bedclothes and called her name and started to talk to her. She was lapsing in and out of consciousness. Sometimes she opened her eyes wide and said: "Who?"

"Sue!" I said.

"Sue," she repeated.

And then she tried to speak but only managed two or three words at a time. It became clear she knew me and was very pleased I was there. The more I talked the more responsive she became and was certainly hearing my voice. Then she would drift off again. She was making every effort to communicate with me. As I looked at her I knew this was the last time I would see her. She may be gone in hours rather than days, I thought.

But God used that time so well…so beautifully. How glad I am that He'd dealt with me and I was just available. This *was* a matter of life and death.

I talked to her. I took her back to when we first met. I reminded her of the time she asked me why I was so happy and contented, always with a smile on my face, and whatever I had she wanted! I reminded her of my answer that I had a Saviour and His name was Jesus. I reminded her of her reply that she too would like a Saviour like that, and I said – "You can."

As I talked to her I checked if she was listening and asked if she could remember. I always got a response – a nod or a word. I reminded her of the evening we'd prayed together and she had asked Jesus into her life.

Then I told her what God had said to me after my last visit to her.

I said: "Di, God wants you to know that He took you at your word right from the beginning. He's never rejected you, and despite all your doubts and theological tangles He's held onto you. He knew all your weaknesses but He took you at your word. He understood what it was all about even if you didn't. I'm here today Di because He loves you; Jesus loves you. You know me, Di, I'll always tell you the Truth. You know that I love Him, and you know what a difference knowing Him in my life has made to me. Now I want to share that with you because it is the most important thing for you at this moment – to know Him who loved you enough to die for you so that you could know Him and love Him in return.

"God is showing me that your greatest need right now is to be loved and know you are loved. It's always been your greatest need. You need to know right now how much you are loved – *by someone*. You have a God who loves you and wants to take you in His arms and hold you and comfort you. I love you, Di, simply because He has given me His Love for you."

All the time I talked I touched her hands, massaged her arms and her neck, held her face, and kissed her, and whispered –

"Jesus loves you; I love you."

I could feel her responding. She tried to speak and she smiled. My heart melted; I was so encouraged. I felt that as I ministered the Love of God to her that I had in my heart, the Holy Spirit was doing something even deeper.

"Di," I said, "it's not enough to know *about* Jesus. You need to know Him as your own Saviour. Right now the presence of God is very real. I can feel it. Do you know Him, Di?" A clear nod. "Jesus – do you know Jesus? Has He become real to you?" Again a decisive nod.

"Praise God – just allow Him to love you, Di. Just let Him love you."

At that she opened her eyes, looking straight at me, and started to move the hand I was holding, and kept repeating – "Hand…out, hand…out." I brought her hand out from under the bedclothes. More earnestly she spoke – "Hand out…out."

I said I wasn't sure what she wanted. Did she want her hand lifted up? A nod. I lifted it up and she said – "Yes, yes…" and then repeated – "Hand…out" again.

"Do you want the other hand out, Di?" A 'yes' and a nod. So I rested the hand I was holding up on my shoulder in order to reach across the bed, pull back the bedclothes in order to reach her other hand.

Then it dawned on me what she was getting at!

"Di, you want a hug, don't you?"

A giggle of excitement came from her lips with yet another nod. My heart leapt. I reached for the other hand, bent over and lifted it onto my other shoulder. Then with her two hands on my shoulders I leaned forward and tucked my hands under her very bony back and held her. As I went forward both her hands slid down my back. I put my face right down to hers and cheek-to-cheek we held each other firmly. I kissed her several times and we just lay there for a while. It was a wonderful feeling; I felt so close; we were so close…closer than we'd ever been, and these were the things that mattered. For several minutes it was so peaceful and still. I didn't want to move and I was certainly oblivious to anyone else in the ward. I realised later we were getting some curious looks!

As I sat up she looked so peaceful. The dinner trolley was arriving and it seemed the right time to go. When I spoke to her she looked at me intently, and tried to lift both hands.

"You want another hug?" A big nod.

So once again I put each of her hands on my shoulders and as I leaned down close to her face and put my hands under her back, her hands again slid down my back and she held me and I held her.

I spoke to her: "You know, Di, when you had your hands out to the sides like that it at first it reminded me, just for a moment, of Jesus with His hands stretched out on the Cross because He loved you and me. I've never seen your hands open wide like that before, Di. But I want to say to you earnestly – keep them open wide now for Him – for Jesus. *I'm* hugging you now, but I'm going and I'm going to say 'Goodbye'. But He's right here and He will not leave you. Keep your arms open to Him and let Him take you up into *His* arms. Okay, Di?" I felt a great sigh from her followed by a giggle.

"That's His Joy – enjoy it!"

A bigger giggle.

"I wonder what these people are thinking about us all entwined like this?!"

She kept giggling and I joined her. Neither of us, face to face, in a close embrace could stop giggling.

My last remark – "I'm getting stuck in this position Di…my arms have got pins and needles and my legs are going to sleep!"

Hoots of laughter vibrated against my cheek and through her bony frame. I was awestruck. The Joy of the Lord is an amazing miracle. This was a woman of nearly ninety-one years, semi-conscious, and near to death.

"Where, death, is your victory…where is your sting?"

She didn't really want me to leave but I knew it was right to go. I said 'Goodbye' to her, kissed her and said I loved her. And I left with such a wonderful feeling inside me. What a wonderful God we have. But I also left convinced I would not see her again.

This was Friday lunchtime…

All through the weekend I was anticipating a phone call from Win my neighbour who was the contact person for Di's nephew, relaying any news. The weekend came and went – no phone call. Same on Monday. I made a decision Monday evening to visit the hospital next morning after my hour's work at Quest.

When I woke next morning I decided to ring the hospital and ask if Diane Haney was still there. How could she have survived another four days? I spoke to the sister on duty. She said yes, Di was still with us but everyone was amazed. They had expected her to slip away days ago. But she kept rallying every time they thought she was a 'gonna'!

Sister said: "I don't know what's keeping her going. She's got the constitution of an ox. Realistically she shouldn't still be with us."

I said I'd be in to visit immediately. She gently warned me of Di's condition, and also said that Di had been agitated a little while earlier.

Peter came up with me and decided to come onto the ward for a few minutes because we weren't expecting to see her again. We entered the ward and even though I'd seen her a few days before and clearly dying, that was no preparation for what we saw today. To all intents and purposes we were looking at a cadaver. Her mouth was open wide, her skin taut across skeletal bone, her eyes not fully closed but lost up into her upper lid. I touched her face, head, and neck – all felt solid as concrete. And yet she was still breathing, and the nurse reckoned that although she couldn't speak she could hear and had some awareness of people coming to her.

I breathed a silent – 'Thank You Lord.'

I didn't at first look at Peter. I knew he had to adjust to what he saw. I asked him to move her table so that I could sit on her bed. I pulled back her blanket and reached for her hand, took hold of it and squeezed it.

"Di...it's Sue, I'm here."

I leaned forward and whispered in her ear and repeated it. She took a deep breath and a long sigh. I kissed her and said I loved her. I sat back down, keeping hold of her hand and continually massaging it and her lower arm. I touched her face again gently, her cheeks, her chin, her neck. I couldn't take my eyes off her, and I could feel the shock draining energy out of me. At the same time a strong compassion rose up within me. I knew she needed the contact and comfort that I could bring right at that moment.

I cast a couple of glances at Peter – he was clearly shocked too, and there were tears in his eyes. That shook me even more because he had nursed in a geriatric hospital. I looked at him and realised you can never really get used to this. He suggested her lips were dry and we looked around her cupboard for the appropriate swabs. I dipped them in some water and moistened her lips.

Peter decided to leave and go up to another ward in search of an old nursing friend. Before he left he gave such a timely word of encouragement. In response to the comment about whether she was really aware of our presence, he said:

"Oh yes, she's aware of your presence all right, and she's very happy about it."

When I asked him how was he sure, he replied:

"I've been observing and I've seen her responses. She *is* aware of you and you are doing a lot of good, be sure of that."

After Peter had left I sat with her quietly, just holding her hand. I began to relax in the Lord and the feeling of shock began to wear off. I just allowed the presence of God to touch me. I prayed quietly in tongues and the Peace of God settled in my soul. My mind began to clear and I was quiet enough to hear from God. I began to realise why I was here. There was unfinished business.

I remembered my earlier conversation with Sister – Di kept rallying round; they didn't know what she was holding on for. Now God was telling me she was holding on because she wouldn't let go…couldn't let go, and that is why he had brought me in at this moment. I listened to Him and I spoke to her as I listened.

"Di, it's decision time. It's time to let go and trust God with your life. You've lived a very long and independent life, made all your own decisions and been in control. Even when taken ill in the past and brought into hospital, you've chosen to take yourself off home against doctors' orders. Di, it's time to face it – you are no longer in control. There are no other decisions to take now except one – to trust Jesus. Put your life into His hands right now, Di. You asked Him to be your Saviour twenty-two years ago, but you always kept control; you never surrendered your life to Him, and you missed out a whole load of blessings.

"This is crunch time, Di. You know He loves you, and you know what I am saying is right. He's waiting right here, so close. There's no better place for you to be right now than in the arms of the Saviour. Let go and stop struggling; let go and *trust* Him, Di. Leave the final decision to Him. When you do that He will do one of two things – He'll either take you straight to Glory with Him, or He will raise you up from this bed and heal you, and you'll be running around this ward restored and with a great testimony to share. He can do it, believe me, He can do it. Either way would be wonderful, Di. Either way is better than where you are right now. It's time to make your last decision and hand your life over to Him and let Him choose what He will do. *Trust Him Di, and make Him Lord.* Trust him *now;* you don't have to suffer any longer."

I sat quietly again, slowly taking in what I had said to her…amazed at what I had said to her, but with such peace that I had simply shared what God had put on my heart, from His heart. I looked at her and believed she was responding and that the peace I felt was covering both of us. I was so grateful that I know Him, really know Him.

I knew it was almost time to go. I realized I'd done what I'd been sent to do this morning, and I also believed that with Di at the wonderful age of nearly ninety-one, He was going to take her home, not just physically healed, but take her home and for her that would be His very best. I also knew that if what I sensed was right it would be but a very short time before she left.

I remembered the hugs we shared the last time. I looked at her and thought – not possible this time.

'Yes it is,' was the whisper within.

So I slowly pealed back the bedclothes, slid one arm under her arm and around her back, and the other arm around her neck. Then I leaned forward and at the same time eased her away from the bed slightly. I was thrilled to feel her arching the small of her back to help me get a grip! We hugged and I told her Jesus loved her and I loved her, and that in His arms was the most wonderful place to be. I laid her back down gently and looked at her. All her struggling seemed to have stopped, and there was a tremendous look of peace across her face. I repeated the process and again she tried to help by raising the small of her back away from the bed. I cannot explain in words what joy that was to me.

I said my goodbyes and left her just after midday. I met Peter for coffee in the hospital café. We chatted and I shared a little with him, and then we made our way home for a late lunch. I was now waiting for the phone call. I knew it wouldn't be long. My old friend Di had nothing to hold on for now. I truly believe by the Grace of God she found the way to let go and let God take control.

The call came two hours later, just after she had died. To me she had just let go and left, her body an old suit she no longer needed. Now she was with Jesus. And I thank Him for breaking through all my assumptions and doing it His Way.

Chapter 20

DEEP CALLS TO DEEP

Deep calls to deep in the roar of your waterfalls;
all your waves and breakers have swept over me.
Psalm 42:7

'**T**OUGH TIMES...EVERYTHING FEELS TOUGH' – is an excerpt from my diary one day in 1995. At home and at church everything was hard going.

"It's your age," older relatives and friends who had gone through the menopause offered! Even the doctor thought it was hormonal fluctuations causing up and down stress levels and heart irregularities; later the latter was discovered to be angina caused by blocked coronary arteries and two leaking heart valves.

My diary continued: 'I'm not clinically depressed but have awful ups and downs emotionally; and the heart thing – very frightening at times. It suddenly clears and everything quietens down; days, sometimes weeks of turbulence and then suddenly PEACE. I have no control over it. My self-confidence takes a battering. One minute I'm full of the joys...full of life and vitality, getting things done. Then I start to wind up, can't concentrate or think straight. Short-term memory is terrible and I can't seem to cope with the things I normally sail through.

'It's a wilderness spiritually too. The tangible sense of God's presence isn't there. I don't doubt it, but at this time especially I long for the past experiences of the warmth, the overwhelming waves of Love, the supernatural Peace and the wonderful sense of security that accompanies the intimate feeling of His Love and Presence. Lord, it's now that I need it! My faith seems to be growing in spite of the lack of tangible evidence, but I feel so lonely, so empty, without the sense of Father's arms wrapped around me.'

It's Friday and I'm walking Boris across the fields. I've felt like a tight coiled spring all day, with accompanying tightness in my chest, radiating left and right up into both sides of my neck. When I'm like this then walking up a slight incline feels as though I'm climbing Everest.

As usual I pray as I walk. I talk so much over with the Lord that I double back around the fields again – I feel there is unfinished business and I need to give myself more time and space. Boris, of course, loves the extra walk. Coming to my usual exit point through the woods I decide to turn left and keep walking –

"Jesus, I love You…I love You." Tears well up…and yet I'd been so tense for days that I hadn't been able to cry. I say it again –

"Jesus, I love You." The words seem to be wrenched up from deep down somewhere. I was speaking what was true and purified, and with an ache and a longing I don't understand.

At times of great difficulty I always tell Him I love Him; I know I mean it; the words always seem to be accompanied by the same ache and longing. It's not a cry for help – that's different. It's just an expression of truth…not feelings, because my feelings are not operating properly in the midst of the storm and the stress and the anxieties.

"I don't understand Lord. Why, when I am in the midst of such turmoil, distracted by turbulence and fears, self-concerned and preoccupied...unwillingly so – why, instead of crying for help, do I find myself expressing such love for You? I don't understand, Lord – where does it come from? It comes out of my mouth yes, but seems to dredge up through all the debris and comes out purified in the process. Why Lord?" I hear –

'Deep calls to deep' and *'I've told you I will never leave you nor forsake you.'*

I stop in my tracks...and ponder on what I've heard, and begin to understand...something.

"Deep calls to deep – You mean, Lord, that it's my spirit saying 'I love You' – my spirit, not my flesh? For I know that my flesh and my soul are in turmoil. The words are coming out of my mouth, but it's my spirit telling You I love You?"

'Yes.'

"But there's more isn't there, Lord? What is it?"

'Deep calls to deep.'

Revelation begins to dawn – my spirit is the *deepest* part of my being. "It is my spirit that is born again...has come alive...is indwelt by your Spirit, Jesus – the Holy Spirit. You live inside me by Your Spirit. My spirit and Your Spirit are knit together, joined, united deep in my being...betrothed. All that You have been revealing, Lord, about the Bride and the Groom, the Church and the Lamb, the believer and Jesus Christ, it is a spiritual union awaiting the day of consummation. My spirit is the essence of me, *is me,* the real me, and is in deep communion with the Holy Spirit. Wow Lord, there is a permanent, eternal and intimate living relationship going on inside me between me and You, *in the Spirit.* My spirit is pure; the enemy can't touch it...it's where I'm united with You. All this disruption going on in the rest of me is temporary and will pass away…it indeed has the mark of death on it. But the *real* life is already mine and going on at a much deeper level. So when this turmoil is going on and I'm feeling weak and lonely and fearful and…

"My true relationship with You is operating on the spiritual level, and at the moment my soul and body are not able to enjoy it all. At *this* level I'm missing out, not enjoying all the fun of such a wonderful relationship, and seemingly missing You too, Lord.

"DEEP CALLS TO DEEP – My spirit is saying to Your Spirit – 'Jesus I love You.' Coming from deep down the expression of my heart and spirit comes up, breaks through the debris and comes out of my mouth."

'From the abundance of the heart the mouth speaks.' True words from the lips of Jesus in Matthew 12:34.

"Amen, there's more I see now, Lord. I've always said I could never have loved You if You hadn't first shown Your Love for me. It was Your Love that drew my love. My love for You is, and always will be a response to Your initiative. So, Lord, if my spirit is saying – JESUS, I LOVE YOU – then that too, I believe, is simply a response to Your Spirit saying to my spirit – SUE, I LOVE YOU. And this mutual expression of love is going on continually despite the turmoil and the distractions on the surface.

"The REAL Life is going on at the spiritual level, Lord, and this is the Life that will continue in Glory. No wonder You exhort me in Your Word – *walk in the Spirit…live by the Spirit, not in the flesh."*

'I told you I'd never leave you nor forsake you, Sue.'

"Of course not, Lord. It's impossible – I see that now."

I kept walking, tears freely flowing out of overwhelming love and gratitude for my Jesus, my Saviour…my LORD. It was as though a light had been switched on, surrounding me with a warm glow. And I could *see* what I had known in my head but had never seen before with my heart and spirit. I felt so grateful; I felt a tremendous liberty. I must learn to walk in the Spirit, and in a Godly freedom, regardless of what is going on in the flesh.

"Help me Lord, and thank You."

I arrived yet again at the point where I exit through the woods. I had come to feel really apprehensive about the slope up into the wood that faced me. It was one of those places that felt like Everest! This time I stopped for a couple of seconds, and then felt the Lord's nudge –

'YOU CAN RUN IT.'

Never hesitating, I took off at a gallop up the slope, through the wood, down the path and across the cradle bridge. I only stopped to put the lead on Boris. And then I kicked up my heels and off I ran again down the road to home. How exhilarating! Did I feel good? Yes – I was feeling free. Where had all this heart trouble gone…the breathlessness, the tightness, the feeling of faintness, and the fear of the strain?

I hadn't had any 'deliverance' ministry. I'd had 'revelation' ministry! And one of the consequences of this fresh revelation from Jesus was I was free from something. What? Fear? Probably, but there was more, and time will tell. I wasn't fretting anymore…just enjoying!

Chapter 21

GO, I AM SENDING YOU

For you shall go to all to whom I send you, and
whatever I command you, you shall speak.
Jeremiah 1:7 NKJ

BACK IN 1977 when, as a brand new Christian, I went forward in a YWAM tent meeting for prayer for 'power to witness' (see Ch. 6), a challenge was given that probably stopped most people in their tracks to re-assess their reason for going forward. Was the challenge intended to separate those who wanted to play with the gift of tongues and those seriously determined to go anywhere in the world for Jesus as His witnesses? The former could mean staying in the comfort of your own home with a new richness and power to one's prayer life. The latter could mean going places that were scary, far away from home, and even dangerous.

And the challenge, to quote my own words:

'Only come forward those who are ready to surrender their lives to the Lordship of Jesus Christ, and be ready to go anywhere in the world He may choose to send them...even Russia.'

I didn't want to go to Russia, still deep in the dark shadows of communism. It was a frightening thought. But I was consumed with the desire to 'go' for God and be a witness for Jesus. Right at that moment my fears were under the thumb of faith, and I committed myself, my husband and our children to God and told Him that if He wanted me to go to Russia then I was willing.

That was in September 1977. Although I knew I could witness for Jesus on a one-to-one basis or in small groups, and indeed saw fruit born to the Glory of God, and even got a buzz doing door-to-door work with the church…though that was a bit scary, I was limited geographically because of fears. From the moment I was born again the Holy Spirit got to work first on the lesser fears, and then went deeper and deeper. But I was still not free and I pleaded with God with many tears and anguished cries.

The closer I got to Him and the more my love for Him grew, the more desperate I was to be free. I started to deal with the fear that bound me more strongly than any other – the phobia about vomiting. It meant I was not comfortable eating anywhere else than my own home. I couldn't go out to hotels and restaurants, and even felt terrified going out to friends for an evening meal. It was sheer torment. So what was the actual fear? Well, it was having food in my mouth and not being able to swallow it in case I choked on it and died. When it began to dawn on me that it was ultimately a fear of death I was angry that I, a child of God, could be held in such bondage by the enemy. I was ready to do serious business with God and wanted Him to help me be freed from this tyranny in my life.

Until I was free, travel was restricted; I certainly couldn't go abroad if God wanted to send me…and Russia was out of the question! We spent all our holidays, until the children were well into their teens, in caravans, self-catering. I was comfortably in control of that; and our favourite place was on a working farm in North Cornwall. The kids loved it and so did

Peter and I. We were such regulars that we were treated to a free week at the October half-term holiday!

My confidence began to grow slowly as God answered my desperate prayers in His way. Peter and I had our first holiday abroad when we took forty children on a school trip to Holland back in 1969. I enjoyed many parts of that trip but eating was a nightmare and I came very close to a breakdown trying to keep smiling *and* keep a lid on the fear.

In February 1990, twelve years after my conversion, we went off to Mallorca for a week. We had a great time and I was able to enjoy the food. There was a mixture of Spanish and English food, and a little German as well to cater for German guests. I was willing to try everything; Peter was a bit more conservative. He did however try the 'elastic bands' in batter, and when the next day I asked what they were and was told 'calamares' – i.e. squid – Peter went a bit pale and said: "Never again," but I tucked into some more.

I felt freer than I had felt for a very long time. But it didn't last. After a couple of months I was aware of bouts of apprehension when going out for a meal. It didn't feel exactly as before, but similar symptoms of the phobic fear of vomiting when eating, started to be growing back again.

I cried out to God: "Why Lord, why? I thought I was free from this."

I heard clearly His reply:

> *'We have thus far dealt with branches. But for you to be totally free the roots need to be dealt with too. Will you trust me in this?'*

I sensed that God was treating this as serious business, that He wanted me to go much deeper and needed me to be willing to go all the way with Him to be free. When I asked Him if this was so He confirmed it. I took a deep breath and agreed:

"Do what you have to do, Lord. I want to be free, really free...so free that I will be able to go wherever you tell me to go, taking whatever you give me to give away, wherever you send me."

And so over the next couple of years God gently led me on towards that freedom I so longed for. There were difficult times, very frightening times mixed with times of great blessing and joy. Finally, just before going on holiday to Spain, I knew the time was ripe for ministry. So I asked three fellow church leaders, who were also close friends in the Lord, if we could arrange a time to meet for ministry with me, giving us all time to be well prepared in prayer and seeking God concerning my situation. The details of that ministry are for another time...another book perhaps. But that day I was gloriously delivered from a stronghold of the enemy in my life that, like a cancer, had put roots down and grown strong from a very early age. God did the complete job that He promised, and I was at last free, and have never been troubled by that problem again.

Free to go and I have gone...now I am a pensioner and I am still ready to go! It wasn't ability I was lacking, for God had gifted me...it was availability, and ability without *availability* meant God can't use me or you in His service. Now free from fears, where did He say *'Sue, go'*?

Very early in my Christian walk the Scripture at the top of this chapter reverberated right through me. My spirit leapt as I recognised God speaking to me as I read this passage about the call of Jeremiah. But my body and soul cringed with fear at the thought of taking God seriously here and, like Jeremiah, I tried to get away from it:

> *"Lord I do not know how to speak, I'm only a child in the faith." v.6.*

But as with Jeremiah the Lord said to me:
'Do not say "I am only a child". You must go to everyone I send you to, and say whatever I command you to. Do not be afraid of them...' – v.7. Afraid? That's exactly how I felt, and I was still a number of years away from freedom.

Then *v.17 – 'Get yourself ready. Stand up and say to them whatever I command you. Do not be terrified or I will terrify you before them.'*

Gulp! I swallowed heavily. 'Terrified?' It hadn't taken much to terrify me. At the time what God was saying to me was impossible. For someone whose hands and feet sweated profusely, eyes blurred and knees shook when I read a passage of Scripture in church or was asked to share briefly about something, only God could help me – I was sure of that. But I reckoned He was on my case and miracles were His business, and miracles were what I needed to transform my life!

I loved the Scriptures; I loved reading them out loud in my daily quiet time; I loved teaching myself what they meant, and my prayer partner, Jane, graciously let me bend her ear almost daily as I excitedly shared fresh revelation from the Word of God with her. My confidence grew to share and teach the Word from the back row in the prayer meeting or home group. I would be very anxious, nevertheless, if asked to prepare the study and lead the meeting. But God was very patient. I began to realise, and others began to confirm, that God had given me a gift of teaching, and I was now exercising that gift in a small way and in a safe environment. I loved doing it. My love for God grew, and for His Word, and His people, and a hunger grew to be able to touch lives with the Word of God outside the fellowship.

Suffering from angina attacks, pain, and breathlessness in my late 40's, and being diagnosed with severe premature coronary heart disease at forty-nine was quite a blow. All three coronary arteries were badly blocked, with also two leaking valves, a heart murmur, and an enlarged heart muscle. I had been eager to get up and 'go' with my new freedom. Now I was stopped in my tracks...and if the devil had had his way I would have been stopped *dead* in them. My doctor told me:

"You have unstable angina; if you are in any trouble don't come to me...go straight to the hospital." More recently he commented that it was a miracle that I never had a heart attack at the time. I replied that a heart attack on one of the blockages would have killed me because they were all blocked high up, and a coronary at any one site would have taken out a third of my heart and I would probably not have survived. But God hadn't finished with me and wasn't ready for me to go home to Glory just then. So yes, it was a miracle and He was healing me.

When I first asked people to pray for my healing, a quiet unassuming new member of the church, who didn't know me, came up to me one Sunday and said:

"Sue, God spoke to me clearly when I was praying for you this week, and he said He was going to heal your heart – but it would be a gradual work because He had a deeper work to complete too."

I understood and knew in my spirit that she had heard aright. I was so encouraged; I shook off the grave clothes the devil was beginning to wrap around me, and from that moment constantly declared day after day the Scripture God had given me the week before from the Psalms –

"I will not die but live, and I will proclaim the Mighty works of God."

He was teaching me to proclaim Life over myself. And the Word of Life is the greatest antidote to the spirit of death that settles over the sick at times. And yes, there were times when I recognised a spirit of death settling over me. But I knew that God had plans for me, so I would declare that Scripture with authority and tell the enemy where to go. There were times when I went into church on a Sunday morning and my lovely friend and prayer partner, Thelma, would come up and would ask how I was. I would smile and say, "Fine, God is good," or something similar. And she'd look at me and say:

"No, you're not okay. I can see a spirit of death hovering over you."

I nodded. She would wrap me in her arms and pray quietly, but with the sort of authority and anointing from God that the enemy fears and slinks away from. And I would be back in the sunshine. She always demonstrated availability to God and still does and was and is always both a challenge and encouragement to my own faith. I never stop thanking God for her. She is without doubt a gift from Him. I know she would say the same about me. And that is God's Wisdom – to put together two people who are chalk and cheese, to build one another up *with* their differences. We have both come to the conclusion that he used me to toughen *her* up, and her to soften *me* up!

Medically I had to travel to Guy's Hospital three times for an angiogram and then triple angioplasty, with stents. My last visit was to St Thomas' Hospital for a final check up. The nurse who signed me in was a coloured girl of African descent. She was quiet and seemed reserved compared to the African friends I had experienced! I only saw her again when I was back on the ward, resting. I had had an angiogram to check on the condition of my arteries and to do it the surgeon threads the tube up through an incision in the femoral artery in the groin. It is important that bed rest follows, keeping the leg very still and holding a pad against the incision so it can heal.

The nurse came to see how I was getting on, and when I said my arm was aching trying to keep the pressure on, she went off and came back with a weighted pad, which was great and did the job just perfectly. Checking there was nothing else I needed, she went to leave and then hesitated and came back, pulling the curtain around me as she did.

She said: "I'm not in the habit of doing this, and certainly not whilst at work."

But she felt compelled to speak to me with a word that God had given her for me. I immediately reassured her that I had no problem with that at all and I would be happy to hear the Word. She then told me that God was going to heal me completely. I interjected, "What do you mean – my heart?"(Remembering the first word I'd had a year before, that God was going to heal my heart but He was going to do it slowly because of the deeper work needed also).

"Yes, your heart, but it will be a much bigger healing than just your heart. He is going to do a complete healing in your life. It will be a miracle. You will have such an amazing testimony and He will send you out in the power of the Spirit. Many will be touched by the power of God and saved."

I was overjoyed! I could hardly lie still, though I knew I must. If I didn't I was chancing a fountain of blood erupting from my wound. I thanked her for her obedience and assured her I was so encouraged and overflowing with gratitude to God for using her to speak to me like that – someone I did not know and who knew very little about me apart from what was in my notes for the day. The Word was so right and only God knew. She breathed a sigh of relief; she had no idea how I would react. I could have called for her boss and reported her, and she could have got the sack. But she took a chance with God, and she ended up as blessed as I was!

And so the crisis of a life-threatening disease put my faith through the fire, testing it and purifying and proving it to be genuine. That is how God can use trouble in our lives for good and blessing, and I thank Him without reservation for that time of trial I went through with Him…always with Him. And so He was preparing me for "Go, I am sending you." And He chose the time for the words to be put into action, and for me to start proving big-time that He is as good as His Word, and to start practicing…

The first call came out of the blue from the leader of the women's work in another church. Could I speak at one of their monthly meetings on one of the women of the Bible? Without stopping to think (and God's hand was on that too!) I said:
"Yes. Mary Magdalene. I'll speak on Mary."
And two months later, after the August break from all meetings, I stood up in front of a room full of women. Everything up to this point had been a step of faith. I'd prepared thoroughly in quiet times with the Lord and was excited with what He gave me. But this was nothing new. What was new was I was now about to start sharing in public the blessings I had for so long received in private and hadn't been free to share because of fear.

The most amazing thing happened. As soon as I opened my month...before I was into my second sentence, I actually felt the anointing of the Holy Spirit descend and rest upon me. Words are inadequate to describe it – but it was pure Peace, a fragrance in my nostrils, a surging wave of Love and power right through me...Love for God and Love for the ladies in front of me. And as I continued to speak, Joy kept breaking forth and touching them as well. Absolute freedom like I'd dreamed of. This was a first...a new experience, and an indication that God had called me to use my mouth for Him and teach the Word of God, and touch lives for Him. And He also showed me what Prophecy was in the context of encouraging and building up the Body of Christ – with this specific Word I finished with, which He had given me for them concerning the teaching I had brought on Mary Magdalene:

"I want the heart that she had for Me to be the heart that you have for Me. It's your heart I want, says the Lord...your love, your affection. I love each one of you with an everlasting Love, no one more or less than the other. It is My Covenant Love for you, which I will never break. But it's your response that makes all the difference. For there to be a deep relationship there has to be a mutual love for one another. I've put My Spirit within you and now My desires lie deep within too. I don't ask you to strive – but to surrender... surrender to the inflow of My Love. Just ask Me and I will do it, and then you will know... you will understand, and there will be nothing to stop the outpouring of YOUR love for Me. You see, it was My Love that purified her heart, and it is the pure in heart who will see their God. When SHE saw she understood, and when she understood she responded and poured back to Me all that I had given to her. And in so doing she fulfilled the greatest

longing of My own heart – that which drove Me to create man in My image in the beginning; for indeed I chose you from the foundation of the world, IN LOVE, in My Beloved Son. I sent Him to redeem His Bride. He gave everything for her. This Mary was the first to understand, and she gave everything to Him. This is My Word, says Jesus. Now open your heart to My redeeming Love, for I am coming... I am coming soon for My Bride. Let My Love do that purifying work in YOUR heart. Open your heart to Me and you will see, and you will know, and you will understand."

Chapter 22

ON THE MOVE WITH GOD

Go into all the world.... My Presence will go with you, and I will give you rest. Mark16:15, Exodus 33:14

SO DID I GET TO RUSSIA? Yes I did – twice, praise God! But let's carry on from where I finished the last chapter, for God was so gracious and gentle and patient with me as He moved me along with Him in *His* own time and way.

Some months later the phone rang and I was being invited to speak to the ladies' group in the neighbouring church again, and this time I could bring whatever the Lord gave me to bring. I said I'd pray and I did, and God gave me a word, so I rang back and said yes I'd love to come. A few weeks later I was standing again before a roomful of ladies. I was confident about the Word I had prepared, and I was aware of a buzz in the room…a sense of expectation from the ladies and also in my own heart.

I spoke on 'Daughters of the King. Wow! What an Inheritance!'

Again there was an anointing on the Word God had given me and an anointing on the gathering to receive. And there was a freedom –

'Where the Spirit of the Lord is there is freedom,' said Paul to the Corinthians. God had set me free, really set me free to open my mouth for Him. Fear had no place in this. I was

overwhelmed by the blessings and encouragement that not only came to me from Him personally but I received also from seeing Him pouring out His blessing on those ladies.

And He gave me another specific Word for them, too, so we were learning together more about the gift of prophecy to build the church, and once again I record it here to build you up:

'Tell them:

'I want them to know that I love them without measure; that I chose them IN LOVE, in My Beloved Son, from the foundation of the world. That's how long I have loved them. I chose them for myself – to be My children, children of the Living God. I want them to realise as never before the extent of My Love in sending My Son to rescue them. I chose them FOR My Son – to be His everlasting companion, His Bride.

'He showed the extent of HIS Love for them by restoring their relationship with Me... severed by sin. Oh, what price separation was in that moment in time when He was suspended between earth and Heaven. But oh what joy I have in My Father heart as I see the results of His accomplishment. I see those I chose, My children, free to come to Me and say, "Father." I long to hear that. I long to lavish My Love upon them, but why are they reluctant? All that is My Son's is theirs, but why do they hold back?

'Tell them I love them.

'Tell them I long for them to draw closer to Me, to know Me, really know Me; to let Me pour out My Love and gifts upon them: not to be afraid; not to hold back. I have a Father heart wide open and waiting for them to come. All that is My Son's is theirs – an inheritance beyond measure. I long for them to draw upon it for themselves, being transformed by it and being

set free to take the riches of God into the world, to share with those who live in such poverty.

'But for the most part My own people themselves live in poverty too and have no riches to share and therefore don't go.

'How My heart grieves – I want YOU to know who YOU are; how much you are loved; who it is who loves you and lives in you. I want you to know the abundant riches of My Son's inheritance – how to receive it and how to live in it; and how to give it away. Then ALL the Glory returns to Me, says the Lord, and My blessings will abound on My people and into this beautiful world that I made and love.'

A couple of months later the Lord took me a step further on what was becoming quite a journey of obedience to 'Go, I AM sending you.' I was sitting at the table at the back of church one Sunday morning as 'duty leader.' I was part of the joint pastoral leadership team led by Roy, who was preaching.

God gave me a moving picture. It was something very familiar to me because of my sporting past. The scene was at a big athletics meeting at the start of the one hundred metres sprint. The athletes were waiting to be called up to their blocks. Some were standing very still, others were moving – either walking up and down or loosening up on the spot. Each person is different in the way he or she prepares for such an event. The three commands that I heard weren't the officially correct ones ("Take your marks," "Set"….*BANG!*). They were what I was familiar with the many times I had run races –"On your marks," – "Get set," – "Go!" In the picture God was showing me there was an accompanying '*BANG*' of the gun. Then the Lord showed me that the start of the Christian life was like those three commands at the beginning of the race. He reminded me that Paul spoke clearly of the race that lay ahead of us and exhorted us to finish the race to get the prize. But to finish the race you have to start it!

He showed me that those three commands were three baptisms at the beginning of our spiritual journey to qualify us and equip us to run the race laid out ahead of us by God Himself.

By this time I was scribbling rapidly in my notebook, making notes of what He was showing me and trying to keep up with Him!

'On your marks' was the first move toward God in repentance by us, and the Holy Spirit responding by baptising us into the Body of Christ – spiritual birth…being born again from above.

Then 'Get set' was our next step of obedient preparation for us to live fully for God. And that is being baptised in water by another Christian (usually a leader), our public confession that we have turned to Christ, died to our old life, been buried in a watery grave, and risen to a new life in Christ.

Then 'Go' (with the bang of a gun!) is the explosive power of coming out of the blocks and starting the race. This is being baptised with the Holy Spirit by Jesus. John the Baptist clearly declared that Jesus would baptise us with the Holy Spirit and with Fire. And Jesus, before He descended into Heaven, warned His followers not to try and operate without this baptism.

He said in *Acts 1* – *'When the Holy Spirit comes upon you, you will receive power and you will be My witnesses.'* Like the explosiveness of the gunshot for coming out of the blocks, Jesus used the word *dunamis* in the Greek to describe the power they, and we, would receive in order to come out of the spiritual blocks for Him. And this word translates as 'dynamite' in the English!

An athlete who doesn't obey all three commands will never even start the race. The spiritual parallel God was showing me was just the same. Without obeying those three commands and experiencing those three baptisms we won't get out of the starting blocks with God, or for Him – and we might not even get to the starting blocks.

I was amazed! My heart was thumping with excitement. It was so vivid a picture and such simple powerful teaching, and I was so caught up in it that I had no idea what Roy was preaching on. Then God spoke to me:

> '*I want you to preach to this fellowship what I've shown you.*'

In one sense I knew that wouldn't be a problem for I had written it all down in my notebook. I had a complete sermon prepared. BUT I did have a problem –

"Lord, I don't believe women should preach in church!"

There was no reply.

At the end of the service the deacon who was on duty with me commented on how much I seemed to have got from Roy's sermon, scribbling away non-stop! I explained what I had been doing and my problem.

"Have a word with Roy and see what he says," she said.

Next evening was Leader's meeting at Roy and Margaret's home, and I managed to get Roy alone before the meeting started.

His response was simple and straightforward:

"Well Sue, I would be very careful concerning whom I'd allow to preach in the church, and I certainly wouldn't have any problem with you."

"Don't you have any problem with women preaching in church, Roy?" I enquired.

"No, I don't, and seeing as God has given you a word to bring it doesn't seem that He has either. So I suggest you go and spend some time talking it over with Him, and come back to me when you are ready to do it!"

And so one Sunday in September 1999 I preached my first sermon ever, and it was so right, and there was that anointing again, and the Peace of God confirming His presence.

I seriously thought it was a one-off, but four months later I was up at the lectern again with the notes of the second word that God gave me to bring publicly to the body – 'In the beginning Jesus…Light before Life.' I couldn't help giggling when I saw a little card left on the lectern for me. Sharon our pianist, who is a whiz on the computer, had made a card with a picture on the front of me holding forth at the lectern with great enthusiasm and zeal! Inside were the words:

"So you thought you only had *one* sermon!"

Just a little card, but such encouragement to go on with God.

I've got a file containing all my sermon notes, the most recent being no.70 a couple of weeks ago. I never got into the habit of preaching on a regular basis or on a rota system. Only when God gave me a Word to preach would I offer to bring it. That way I kept my deep dependence on God to provide a willingness to obey when He did, and freshness. In bringing a new Word each time I have never repeated the same sermon twice because there has always been a next time when He has surprised me with a new Word. But with the sermon notes of seventy sermons in a file, there may be a different time and a different place where He may want to use some again.

So what about Russia? Well, our daughter, Christine, who had a call from God at the age of ten to go to Russia, found He was opening a door for her to go almost seventeen years later. She arrived in St Petersburg in January 2001 and she served the Lord there for almost four years before returning to UK.

She invited us to visit her in 2002, and having prayed about it God confirmed it was right and by opening an amazing door. I was surfing the web on the evening of January 1st 2002 when we had an excited call from Chris telling us to go onto the BA website for flights to St Petersburg in June, which was when we were considering going. We did so immediately and found flights for just the right dates and at the ridiculous price of £147 return per person, enabling us to have a twelve-day stay. Peter and I were amazed. Any apprehension about going to such an 'out-of-our-comfort-zone' country was overwhelmed by God choosing a moment to say:

> *'You can see I've opened the door wide for you. Go, I am sending you!'*

Without hesitation we snapped up those tickets at that amazing price, filled in all our details and paid by credit card. The contract was confirmed inside a minute and information was given in an email that the tickets would be sent to us by post in the next few days. Wow!

Two days later we had our tickets in our hands. We couldn't open them quickly enough to double check that the price was right and that the airline hadn't perhaps corrected a mistake and taken a lot more from the credit card...this was fairly unfamiliar ground for us! No, the tickets were exactly as we had bought and paid for them, with the same dates and times, and price. And we were going in the middle of June at the time called 'white nights'. That is midsummer in Russia and for a few weeks in June it never gets dark. The sun sets about midnight; there are a few hours of dusk, and by three in the morning the sun is up again.

Peter and I were happy, over breakfast, to have the tickets and chat about the trip to come. As we were doing so I suddenly had a divine nudge:

'Go and check the web site again.' I excused myself and rushed upstairs and put the computer on. I found the web page and went through the options until I got the page we had booked our flight on. I checked the price and gulped. It was now £1115 per person return for the same flights (I double-checked with our tickets). All the details matched our tickets except the cost! Forty-eight hours after buying our tickets for the giveaway price of £147 we found they now cost £1115.

God had been saying, *'Go, I am sending you,'* and this was further than we had ever been; but He knew our anxieties and He so encouraged us with these tickets...they were a gift from Him, the door had been flung wide and we shouted:

"We're going Lord, and nothing is going to stop us now that You have made it so clear! Hallelujah!" Over the months leading up to the trip I checked again on several occasions, and each time the price stayed at £1115!

It was about a month later when I was still soaking in a renewed and deeper sense of belonging to God that He spoke to me clearly:

> *'I want you to take My Word to encourage My people in St Petersburg.'*

"If You give me a clear Word then I *will* take it, Lord." And He did...and I did! I asked Chris to have a word with her pastor that if he would like me to, I would be happy to preach the Word on the Sunday I would be in St Petersburg. Then I left it in the Lord's hands and took my hands off it. If it was right He would open that door too; if it wasn't, He would keep that door closed.

The door was opened wide. The pastor of the Russian church, and his wife, welcomed us with open arms and were a great encouragement. The day after we arrived the Lord confirmed, in a delightful and powerful way, the Word He'd given me to bring. We were taken by Metro into the centre of the city for some sightseeing. St Petersburg is the most beautiful city I have ever seen. I saw more of it on a second visit two years later, because this particular day I noticed most of the big buildings were covered by scaffolding and huge dust sheets. What a shame, their glory covered like that! I asked Chris why? Her answer shook me to the core of my being. She said it was the big clean up of the city in preparation for Jubilee. Next year it would be three hundred years since St Petersburg was built, and there would be a Grand Jubilee Celebration.

I walked ahead of Peter and Chris, overwhelmed with joy, tears welling up, and praising God in tongues as I walked. I didn't want to say anything until I spoke in church on Sunday. Why the joy? Well, the Word God had given me for this church in St Petersburg was: *Jubilee...The Year of God's Favour.*

God knew about their Jubilee preparations...I didn't! So when I brought them the Word about a spiritual Jubilee they were with me all the way paralleling the physical and the spiritual, hungry to be right with God for His blessings in the year of His favour for them. It was electric and I saw His anointing upon that gathering as I looked out upon them.

That had been quite an adventure and I settled back into a routine once back home. It was summertime and I liked to potter around in the garden. Later that year, November 2002, I spent a month in Rhyl, North Wales, on a 'Leader as a Person Course' with OM. That was a tough but rewarding and life-changing experience. But God said, '*Go!*' and He knew that it would have faith-stretching consequences far beyond the limits of the course.

That autumn Jim, a friend and co-pastor with us at Highfield Community Church, suggested that the other two leaders and I consider ordination. He belonged to an international leader's fellowship based in America and had been ordained there. He was and still is an international speaker with a pastoral/apostolic ministry, and he found that being ordained opened doors that may not otherwise be opened. He recognised a call of God on all our lives that could be taking us further afield, and that was why he was suggesting we consider ordination.

I must confess I dismissed the idea; I just wasn't interested. Six months later he brought up the subject again and asked us if we had considered it. Apparently ordinations took place at the Autumn Annual Conference. There was quite a strict process to go through, vetting, affirming ministry and God's call, and interviews. So some notice needed to be given by applicants. My only comment at that time was that I practised a simple way in prayer about 'doors'. I would, on specific issues, ask God to open the door if it was right and close it if it wasn't. Being set free, and willing to go where He wanted me, I found this worked well.

Having dismissed it out of hand the first time, but because I respected Jim and his insight, and his ability to develop leadership gifting in others, and His own ministry blessed by God, I promised I would pray and seek a definite response from God, which is what I should have done in the first place. But I was recognising that I had some hang-ups from my background and upbringing. So to prayer I went, confessing the hang-ups and asking the Lord about this matter and waiting upon Him, confident that He would answer in His way and His time. This was the end of February 2003.

On March 7th I was lying in bed in that half-awake stage before rising…often my best time to hear from God and often at this time of day He catches me unawares with a Word for a sermon. Today was one of those days. Being repeated over and over in my brain were the words –

'Forget the former things…See, I am doing a new thing…do you not perceive it?'

All of a sudden I was awake. I jumped out of bed, sat at my desk and opened my Bible at Isaiah 40-something. I knew it was there somewhere. I found it in *chapter 43:19 –*

'See I am doing a new thing! Now it springs up; do you not perceive it? I am making a way in the desert and streams in the wasteland.'

I wrote it down in my notebook and went and had a shower and got up.

Morning after morning I woke with these words in my head. I got up each time and meditated on the Scriptures and God started giving me thoughts to write down with the Scripture. By now I believed He was giving me teaching for a sermon for church, but I began to realise it was for further afield than the local church, but where?

March 17th I wrote in my diary a passage of Scripture that God used to speak so clearly to my spirit that I felt I was on a path I could not turn back from without surely knowing I would be walking in disobedience. It was –

'I, the Lord, have called you in Righteousness; I will take hold of your hand. I will keep you and will make you to be a covenant FOR THE PEOPLE and a LIGHT FOR THE GENTILES; to open eyes that are blind, to free captives from prison and to release from the dungeon those that sit in darkness.

'I am the Lord; that is My Name! I will not give My Glory to another, or my praise to idols. See the former things have taken place, and new things I declare; before they spring into being I announce them to you!' Isaiah 42:6-9.

God was still expanding His Word to me but today was the day when out of that Scripture He spoke prophetically to me. The two words that burned inside of me as I read them are in capitals – FOR THE PEOPLE, and FOR THE GENTILES. Before I could draw breath he said:

'*The people* are My people, Israel. And *the Gentiles* I am sending you to are Russia and America. Within the next eighteen months you will have visited Israel, America and Russia for Me.'

I said nothing, but an excitement was rippling deep inside.

Three days later in my quiet time my daily reading happened to be part of *Isaiah 43*. There are no coincidences with God, are there?! I read: *"All the nations gather together and the people assemble." V.9.*

Immediately came to mind the Autumn Conference of international leaders of which Jim had spoken, the conference I would be going to if God answered in the positive my prayer about ordination. Now He was saying:

'Take the Word I have given you to this conference.' No mention about ordination, but I had a sermon prepared under the guidance of the Holy Spirit and no, it wasn't for the church in Willesborough. He was telling me to take it to Seattle in Washington State, USA.

I read on: *"'You are My witnesses,' declares the Lord, 'and My servant whom I have chosen.'" v.10*

'Go, I am sending you. I have put My words in your mouth; take them and speak them to the people I send you to, and do not be tempted by men or angels to step outside that calling.'

A week later a handwritten letter arrived in the post from Israel!

"Who do you know in Israel?" my husband enquired.

"I don't," I replied.

When I opened the letter I discovered it was from a woman I'd met the year previously at the course in Rhyl. She'd felt led to invite me to Israel, to bring a group from church that would be willing to work for the Lord with the small team already resident there, willing to be involved in various evangelistic works. It was not a holiday as such but they would be delighted to take us around in their twelve-seater van to places in Israel of our choice. By the end of April nine people attended our first meeting to pray and to plan the trip.

Meanwhile I had spoken to Jim about my speaking at the leaders' conference in America, asking him to speak to Joe McIntyre, the president of IFM, as he, Jim, was the only person I knew who had contact with the leadership there. I knew that this was an impossibility, humanly speaking…a closed door unless the 'boss' sought God in prayer and got an answer from Him. Jim didn't say anything but I sensed he felt this was a non-starter too! But he promised to make the contact on my behalf. Weeks went by and I heard nothing, but I was at peace. It was firmly in God's hands. If I'd made a mistake the door would firmly stay closed. If I was on track with God that door would open wide, and that I felt would be a miracle.

Into May and tentative arrangements had begun to visit Israel the following Easter, in 2004. My God *can* do the impossible. I *am* a very ordinary person, but He *is* without question an extraordinary God. I hadn't heard back from Jim and it was two months since I'd spoken to him. I felt strangely confident that if the president had sought God in prayer then he would say yes to this middle-aged woman, from an obscure place in England, whom he'd never met, knew nothing about; yes to her coming to bring a Word from God, as one of the main speakers in the annual conference.

An email from Jim came in June –

"Book your flights, the answer is yes!"

Chatting to Jim on the phone I asked why it had taken so long. He admitted it was such an unusual request that it was not very likely to happen and he had delayed contacting the president for a while, but eventually put my request to Joe asking him to pray and seek God's will. And Joe did just that and came back to Jim within a week with an affirmative answer. Exciting stuff!

And so at the beginning of October I flew off to Seattle USA and brought to that Fall Conference the Word God had given me back in March, entitled – "Behold I am doing a new thing!" From start to finish, from March to October, the Peace of God ruled in my heart. I was in the right place at the right time, all because God had delivered me from all my fears so I was available to go, and He was my most intimate companion. I loved every minute of it all. I felt loved to bits whilst I was there; the Americans were so warm and friendly and appreciative. And best of all was the fruit I saw as a result of bringing God's Word. There was a lot of serious repentance going on at a personal level with God, people under conviction and wanting to clear out rubbish that had accumulated in their lives, in order to be clean and pure before the Lord and ready to go with Him into the new thing He wanted to do. Serious repentance is always a very healthy sign amongst God's family.

Back in the UK, and the plans for the Israel trip were being fleshed out. We met every month to pray and to plan and there was a real sense of excitement as we entered the New Year of 2004…just a few months to go.

In the midst of all this a message came from Russia via Christine. Ivan and Elena, the pastors in St Petersburg, were asking:

"When is your Mum coming again? Tell her not to leave it too long!"

Suddenly God's Word to me the previous year came to mind:

"Within the next eighteen months you will have visited Israel, America, and Russia for me."

The hairs stood up on the back of my neck. My goodness me, that word is being fulfilled! Given in March 2003, I went to America in October 2003; flights were booked for nine of us to go to Israel in just three months, April 2004; and now an invitation to go back to Russia.

"I wonder when You have in mind for that, Lord."

When I returned from the first trip to Russia I came home with a burden for the Russian women, especially those I'd met in the church. The Truth is that the eyes *are* the windows of the soul, and I saw suffering in the eyes of many women there who loved the Lord. I sought God and He showed me that they had suffered, young and old, from the epidemic of alcoholism in several generations of their men folk – fathers, husbands, sons, brothers. And why such an epidemic? The rule of communism for generations had in effect stolen the authority and headship of a man over his family. The state ruled by fear and many families had been the victims of the 3 a.m. knock on the door by those in power, and their men folk being marched off into the darkness. The women left behind had to be strong for their families, and Russian women are tough! The men felt impotent and of little use to their families as a result of this cruel regime.

It has passed down as a curse through several generations, and even now with communism gone and democracy struggling to get established, the men are turning to alcohol as a result; and women and children living in a home with an alcoholic will be living in an abusive situation. And I saw hurt and brokenness in the hearts of the women I met…suffering from abuse and abandonment from fathers and husbands. And God gave me a burden to go back one day and offer a ladies' day for Him to minister to them as 'Father', loving and compassionate and longing to heal them and take them in His arms as beloved children so they may never feel like orphans again.

I left the timing of my return to Him, and now I was being invited to return. I had originally discussed the possibility with my prayer partner, Thelma, of her doing a ladies' day in Russia with me and asked her to pray about it. She did and knew that God was confirming that. So I contacted her and Garry and asked if they would come to Russia with us. Yes, they could, but they were restricted by times because Garry worked with special needs children in the local secondary school, and could only go in the school holidays. Going in that August, 2004 was okay with all concerned and so we booked our flights and arranged visas.

The details of the trips to Israel and Russia are for another time...another book maybe. But I have discovered that being obedient to God usually means going way out of *my* depth only to discover that He was carrying me in His arms all the time and what a blessing that has been. To know Him intimately as my Father has brought so much healing into my own life. And He would have known of course that I could give away what I had received from Him to those lovely Russian ladies! Actually I found that obedience is always followed by abundant blessings even in difficult circumstances. And to see people ministered to by the Holy Spirit in mighty ways because you are in the right place at the right time brings indescribable joy. God always knows best.

Chapter 23

BOB THE BUILDER

By faith... Abraham was looking forward to the
city with foundations, whose architect and builder
is God. Hebrews 11:10

WE WERE LOOKING for a good and reliable builder
early 2005 to build us an extension on the back of our
house, and there is only one way to avoid the pitfall of
'cowboys' and that is to go by recommendation – to ask around
and have a look at work that has been done. The evidence was
in front of our eyes in a very nicely built two-storey extension
on the semi across the road from us. We were shown around
and given glowing reports about a local builder called Bob
whose handiwork was to be seen in a number of properties in
Willesborough.

So we called him in to discuss the best plan for the space
available and to suit our requirements, which was a small
downstairs bedroom/office with an adjoining en-suite shower,
toilet and washbasin. Plans were drawn up…tweaked here and
there several times, presented to the council and price agreed.

Building work began in earnest at the end of April. Bob the
builder was his own boss with his own business and worked
predominantly on his own, at least in a small job like ours. But
for the first job of digging the footings he hired a mini JCB and
employed a regular partner called Greg for the initial

preparations of footings, laying in the drains, building up to damp course level, and digging out into the garden to extend the patio in front of the extension-to-be, and the building of a keeping wall with steps up into the garden.

Bob was a short wiry man, probably about five foot five, with size five trainers and the strength of an ox. Some of the things I saw him lift on his own would put him in the category of an Olympic weightlifter! He loved his work and I would say he must have had a call to be a builder that was as strong as a Scottish fisherman would describe *his* call to the sea.

When I discovered Bob was in his early sixties I was amazed – he didn't look anything like it. When I said to him –

"Oh no, Bob, when we found a good painter and decorator he was nearing retiring age too, and you'll probably have laid down your trowel before we want to call on you again!"

His speedy reply was – "No, I'm never going to retire. I'll work till I drop."

"Why Bob? Are you afraid of dying?"

"No, it's not dying I'm afraid of, it's becoming an invalid, not being able to do anything for myself and being dependant on someone else to see to all my needs. I'd hate that, and the thought scares me, so I'll just keep going."

"As you know, Bob, I'm a Christian," I replied, "and if you hope to go that quick I think you'd better sort out where you are going afterwards! I'll definitely be praying for you!"

"Thank you. I need that. I believe there's someone up there somewhere looking down on us."

"He certainly is, Bob."

One morning Peter and I got up to find Bob and Greg already at work, on their knees laying the patio. Peter and settled down to breakfast, and I reminded him that it was

National prayer week, and that a woman sitting next to me at work the day before was complaining of severe back pain. So I'd said to her –

"It's National prayer week this week, Jane, would you like me to pray for you?"

"Yes please," she said.

So I put a hand on her back and prayed a brief prayer asking Jesus to heal her.

She broke the silence that followed –

"Wow, thank you, that is really so much better."

"Jesus *still* heals today," I smiled, thrilled and grateful for such an encouraging answer.

Peter looked at me and said – "Go on then!"

I knew what he meant. Help, Lord!

I got up and went into the garden and greeted the builders. I took a deep breath and spoke –

"It's National Prayer week this week. Is there anything either of you would like me to pray concerning?"

"Yes," said Greg immediately, looking up at me. And he got up and came over and shared how worried he was about his wife who was very depressed and had been so since their baby's birth. It was affecting everything they did and he was worn out with worry and the extra struggle it was for them both at home. I just placed one hand gently on his shoulder and started to pray through those things that he had specifically shared, asking Jesus to lift his burden and heal his wife and pour His Love and Peace over the family and home, and make a big difference in that situation. As I prayed his shoulders began to shake and he began to weep as he released his heavy burden. It was as though this had all been bottled up for months and now he was letting it go.

I only saw Greg briefly once more. With the patio finished his work here with Bob was done. But he came up to me at the kitchen door and thanked me for praying. He didn't say anything to his wife but when he got home that evening he found her in a much better frame of mind. She told him she was feeling better and happier than she had for months, and was thinking of going to a local church to see if she could get help.

He was so relieved and grateful and couldn't thank me enough. I thanked him for letting me know the latest news and told him to thank God – He's the One Who answers prayer!

"I certainly will," he said.

That was the last we saw of Greg, but the memory of praying for him is precious and remains in my heart.

Bob continued with the building alone, and apart from bringing in an electrician and a roof felter, he did all the work himself, multi-gifted, and multi-tasking as good as any woman! Periodically in my early morning quiet time I would pray for Bob's salvation, asking Jesus to make Himself known to Him…not to let him die until he knew Him!

The work was well advanced and we were getting excited at seeing the extension take shape. I came in from town one lunchtime and Bob was applying the final layer to the floor. He had had his lunch and we were just having ours whilst he was back working on the floor. I heard him muttering to himself and I shouted through to him – "Are you all right in there, Bob?"

He replied that he didn't have enough of the special cement that he was using for the final surface, and getting more and leaving it to dry for twenty-four hours would add an extra day before being able to get on with the next job. Immediately came to mind the story of Jesus feeding five thousand with five loaves and two fishes, and I thought if He could stretch so little to feed so many, then stretching Bob's cement to finish the floor this afternoon wouldn't be a problem! So I shared with Peter and quietly prayed that the promise in that Word be applied to our 'today' situation. I sat still for a minute and then said to Peter –

"There'll be enough cement, I'm sure of it."

I got back to my lunch but was interrupted by a word from God –

'Tell Bob, you need to activate my promise by speaking it out. You tell him, and I'll do it.'

I had intended keeping quiet and then if Bob later said that the cement went further than he'd expected and the floor was finished, *then* I would tell him I had prayed and God had answered. But God was saying to me –

'You tell him first and then I'll answer. Do you trust me, Sue?'

"Yes, Lord, but you *are* stretching my faith here."

'That's right, how else is it to grow?'

Enough said, and I called out to Bob –

"It's all right Bob, I've prayed about your problem. Don't worry; you *will* have enough cement to finish the floor. If Jesus stretched five loaves and two fishes to feed five thousand, He can keep your cement going till you've finished."

"Right!" said Bob, laughing!

About an hour later after the daily dog walk I went round to the back of the house where Bob was on his knees working on the floor of the extension. Behind him was a wheelbarrow with a spade in it. I got close enough to look in and saw no more than two shovel's worth of cement. Bob still had the area in front of the door and down into the alcove to the left to do, and I would have thought it would take a lot more than two shovelfuls…more like five or six!   But Bob seemed happy enough and was singing away to his music. Perhaps he's got more faith than me, I thought.

Another half hour and I looked again and there was about one shovel-full left. I got him a cup of tea and settled down with mine to watch Countdown.

There was a shout – "That's done!" called Bob.

"What, have you finished?" I called back.

"Yep," said Bob.

I ran out into the back garden. I first looked into the wheelbarrow and there was half a spadeful of cement still in there. I went and stood beside Bob, who was viewing his work, and there was the evidence – the floor was completed.

"Bob, you've still got a bit of cement to spare!" I exclaimed.

"Yep, amazing isn't it?"

"That's answered prayer Bob, God is good!"

"Well, I must admit somebody up there was helping me out."

The whole time he was with us I could feel God's love for this guy, and it was great having him working at our home. The extension was completed to our satisfaction, and the council's, plus a few other jobs done – new front porch, removed unsafe back chimney, replaced a very leaky garage roof, erected some garden fencing, and replaced all soffits, barge boards and drain pipes, living room redecorated. Bob left our premises at the end of July.

We saw him occasionally over the next eighteen months to tweak something here, tighten something there, and to visit various neighbours to do work for them. As I said before, the best man for the job is the one you get as a result of neighbours' and friends' recommendations. I prayed occasionally for Bob whenever he came to mind and when I did it was always the same prayer –

"Lord Jesus, don't let Bob drop dead on the job, unless he has first come to know You as his Lord and Saviour, and knows he is going to spend eternity with You."

It was just coming up to Easter 2007 when I heard the news from a neighbour. Bob the builder had been working on a big project in Deal. He had been feeling ill one morning, and his gang realised he must be really unwell when he asked one of them to drive him home to Ashford. They got as far as the roundabout near the William Harvey Hospital outside Ashford when the driver saw Bob's head drop onto his chest. Bob was not responding; he was either unconscious or dead.

The driver went round the roundabout and back to the hospital stopping the car in the grounds and realised that Bob was indeed dead. He shouted for help. Paramedics arrived and confirmed this and started to work on him there and then. There was zero time to get him into A+E. The usual twenty minutes allowed for resuscitation came and went. Reluctant to carry on, the medics were persuaded to do so by his friend who told them what Bob did and that he was a very strong man.

Forty minutes went by and suddenly a heartbeat was detected. Still unconscious they raced Bob into A+E and continued to work on him and then transferred him to the cardiac intensive care unit. The initial euphoria of bringing him back from the dead after forty minutes – a miracle in itself – was now tempered by the anxiety of certain brain damage. Everyone was hoping against hope that it would be minimal. They kept him under for a while to aid recovery. But when he did come round it wasn't long before he was talking about getting out of hospital and getting back to work. That was nipped in the bud by both his wife and his consultant who said the only work he was going to be doing for the business was at a desk!

Soon up on his feet and taking himself off to the toilet, this man was a walking miracle – having been resuscitated after forty minutes when they normally stop at twenty, and regaining consciousness without any apparent brain damage, apart from the madness of planning a speedy return to work.

They decided to keep him in hospital over Easter and do extensive tests to find out causes for such a massive heart attack and to ascertain what damage had been done in order to treat him and plan for the future.

I was so overwhelmed by God's answer to my personal prayer for this man that I decided to send him an Easter card and I wrote a letter to him and enclosed it with the card –

21st March 2007

Hi Bob,

When you were building our extension you told me you were never going to retire…you would work until you dropped. I prayed then, and since, that you would not die without first being 'saved'. And *you* know Bob, that I believe God answers prayer!

I was shocked at first to hear the news and my immediate question as I was being told was – "Did he die?" The answer was – "Yes he died, but he didn't stay dead. It's amazing, a miracle. They got him back after forty minutes. And he's now recovering well!"

And I thank God for that.

Easter will soon be upon us. How about using some of your recuperating time to consider this year what all that is about, and how it relates to you? For the One who died on the Cross that first Easter, and rose again, is the same Jesus who said – "I am the Resurrection and the Life. He who believes in Me will live even though he dies; and whoever lives and believes in me will never die. Do you believe this?" John 11:25/26.

.   In the Bible Jesus not only healed the sick – He also raised the dead.   And His motive was always compassion.

This life is simply a preparation for the next; and compared to our time in eternity after we die, this life is as short as spitting in the wind.

So, Bob, please don't be eager to die rather than retire until you have settled where you are going to spend the 'forever' afterwards.

"He who calls on the Name of the Lord will be saved."

Try talking to Him. You *will* be surprised!

I wish you a good recovery. Enjoy the moment and may Easter 2007 be a very special one for you and yours.

Every blessing,

Sue (Ross) x

One Saturday morning before I'd had my breakfast and Peter was still in the bathroom there was a ring on the front doorbell. I opened it expecting it to be the postman. But there stood Bob the builder! I was not just surprised to see him there, but amazed to see he was dressed for work…his builder's uniform being the comfortable trainers, blue jeans, check shirt, and the pencil behind the ear!

"I had to just come and thank you for the card and letter you sent me in hospital. I really did appreciate it," he said immediately. He readily agreed to my invitation to come in and have a cup of tea; all the time he worked for us I can't remember him refusing a cuppa. I think that as a car runs on petrol, a builder runs efficiently on a regular flow of tea! I called to Peter that Bob was here and he was out of the bathroom, dressed and downstairs in a couple of minutes. He wanted to see this miracle for himself!

And that was the first thing I said to Bob –

"Well, I'm now looking at a miracle firsthand!"

Obviously I was curious to see him in working gear only a couple of weeks after being discharged from hospital, and asked him what had happened. He related the whole story and the part I had heard had obviously been quite accurately relayed to me and others. Then he explained that they kept him in hospital until they had done all the tests needed and worked out what medication he needed. But the medics were left in a quandary. Despite repeating tests they found no damage to His heart. It was perfectly healthy and there were no signs of the massive heart attack he had suffered and which had affectively killed him. I couldn't help but exclaim –

"Wow, Bob, brought back to life, and then no sign of the heart attack – that's two miracles you've had. God didn't leave you an invalid, did he? He healed you too!"

"Yes, that's right, and everyone is saying I had a miracle, and I truly believe I am being looked after."

"You weren't offended then by what I wrote? I know it was pretty straight stuff."

"No, certainly not. I really did appreciate very much what you wrote, and I want to thank you again."

"I'm thanking God, Bob, it's all His work. He's into miracles. We often miss them...don't see them for what they are. So you look as though you are working?"

"Yes, I'm doing a job nearby, but wanted to call in here first."

"So you are just starting back to work are you, and taking it slowly?"

"No. I've been back two weeks."

"Two weeks! What, full time?"

"Yes. They discharged me and said to take it easy at home; take time to recuperate and build my strength up. I think everyone thought I was going to retire, but when I made it clear I wasn't, I was advised not to go back to work too soon, and the first week to work no more than two days and build it up gradually – perhaps even work part-time, seeing as I was my own boss. But one week at home twiddling my thumbs was enough for me! So I started work again and did two days the first week, like they said. But I wasn't going to mess around like that any longer. So I went straight back full time the next week and I've done two full weeks now."

Remembering the very heavy work he used to do on his own, I asked –

"Does that include doing all the heavy work you used to do as well?"

"Oh yes, back to normal and it's great. I have no problems at all."

"Praise God!" I exclaimed. "I will continue to pray for you, Bob."

"Well, I thank you once again." He smiled. "Now I'd better get over the road – they're expecting me."

"See you again Bob. Bye."

POSTSCRIPT: WHY DID I WRITE THIS BOOK?

*If I say: "I will not mention Him or speak
anymore of His Name,"
His Word is in my heart like a fire, a fire shut up
in my bones.
I am weary of holding it in; indeed, I cannot.
Jeremiah 20:9*

EIGHTEEN MONTHS after my first encounter with God I committed my life to Jesus as my Saviour and was born again. Two days later I surrendered to His Lordship as He baptised me in the Holy Spirit and the power of God came upon me. The next day I opened my Bible and as I began to read, the Holy Spirit's power came upon me again. This happened the next day and the next as I started my morning quiet times. It was as though my love for the Living Word of God was also now branded on my heart, by fire, for the written Word. After a few days I went into town and bought a hard-backed notebook. In the front I wrote notes and meditations as I started to study the gospel of John. In the back of the book I put a heading – 'Personal Witness' – and kicked off with the story of that first encounter with God.

In a matter of months the notes in the front met the testimonies in the back and the book was full. A second hard-backed book was purchased, bigger in size and with more pages. By the third book the notes were in the back and the testimonies in the front. Book five was the biggest book I could find. I never did fill it, *not* because I ran out of things to write, but because I modernised myself from the handwritten word to filling files with *typed* stories and testimonies and wonderful lessons I had learned from the Scriptures.

And now I have gathered together under the hand of God the contents of this book. Why? Well, the evidence is there – from the moment I was filled with the Holy Spirit there was a Divine motivation to write things down. God gave me a mouth and a pen, and the power to use them both for His Glory. Then He gave me a longing for people to be saved and to know Him as I know Him. I am not speaking of uniformity here, for each one is unique and each one is precious, and He meets with each person in a special and unique way. But to meet Him and to get to know Him and to grow in a deep love relationship with Him is the longing He has put in my heart for people both churched and un-churched. He is a Holy God with such a passionate love for His creation that He Himself paid the ultimate price to make reconciliation and such a love relationship with Himself possible for anyone who would respond and love Him in return, trusting Him and walking in obedience with Him.

So I write as a *witness* – that's what Jesus said, at the beginning of Acts, that the power of the Holy Spirit was given for; and I write as a *teacher* declaring with Paul that:

"ALL Scripture is God-breathed, and useful for teaching, rebuking, correcting and training in Righteousness, so that the man of God may be thoroughly equipped for every good work." 2 Timothy 3:16/17.

And I write as an *encourager* to the believer:
"Keep on keeping on with God, for He who said:

"I have loved you with an everlasting Love" (Jeremiah 31:3), also said:

"I will never leave you nor forsake you." (Hebrews 13:5.)

And I write as an *exhorter* to the unbeliever:

"Taste and see that the Lord is good; blessed is the man who takes refuge in Him." (Psalm 34:8.)

But supremely I write and speak desiring to give God the Glory for who He is to me and for all the things He has done. And the last Word is His Word:

"You are My witnesses," declares the Lord, "and My servant whom I have chosen, so that you may know and believe Me and understand that I AM He. Before Me no god was formed, nor will there be one after Me. I, even I, AM the Lord, and apart from Me there is no saviour. I AM the Lord; that is My Name! I will not give My Glory to another or My Praise to idols." (Isaiah 43:10 and 42:8.)

Yea and amen!